224b and the clerks and staff of the magistrate's office. They (the officers and inhabitants) must accept the aforementioned person as magistrate of that place. They must recognize that the duties and customary rights of that position belong to him.

They are to know that there are strict injunctions in this matter.

Notes

1 Both the terms *kotwāl* and *chabūtara* (for establishment) are Hindi or Prakrit terms for an office which long antedates the Muslim conquest in South Asia. A number of officials in the Emperor's entourage were engaged solely to administer the moving city of the massive imperial camp. They accompanied the person of the Emperor whether he was on tour in camp ("the Stirrup of Felicity") or settled in a city. When the imperial household and the central administration settled in a city for a time, these officials often took over the urban offices as well – thus *kotwāl* of the Stirrup and the city. I am grateful to Stephen Blake for this observation.

2 The purely Islamic office which comes closest in its secular functions to some of the duties of the Indian *kotwāl*, is that of the *muḥtasib*, often translated as "censor", who regulated markets and tried to control the usage of wine and intoxicating drugs and other forbidden acts. Aurangzeb reinstated the office of *muḥtasib*, along with other sweeping policy changes, to make Mughal administration follow the *Sharīʿa* or Islamic law as closely as possible. In 1072 A.H./A.D. 1660 the Emperor issued a general order prohibiting the use of wine, *bhāng* (a beverage made from hemp), and other intoxicants. The newly appointed *muḥtasibs* and other executive officers in the empire were to enforce this edict. For a copy of the edict, *see* Ali Muhammad Khan, *Mir'āt-i Aḥmadī*, translated by M. F. Lokhandwala, number 146 in Gaekwad's Oriental Series (Baroda/[India], 1965), pp. 222–223. According to Muhammad Bakhtawar Khan, writing in the *Mir'āt al-ʿĀlam*, Aurangzeb issued this edict at the time of his second coronation. *See* Sajida S. Alvi, ed., *Mir'āt al-ʿĀlam*, vol. 1 (Lahore, 1979) published by the Research Society of Pakistan.

224b

Position of Appraiser and Headman[1]

At this time the position of appraiser of ______ *maḥals* is transferred from ______ and conferred upon ______, so that he may fulfill the duties and customary obligations of that position with rectitude and propriety.

He must assess accurately the value of the goods that the merchants of those *maḥals* bring in so that no future investigation will reveal any discrepancy. Thereby the officers of that place according to the valuation may collect the (proper) revenues from that (merchandise) for the exalted state. Apart from the established rate, he must not take anything from the merchants. Having satisfied the merchants by his upright conduct, he must not embezzle or falsify even the slightest amount. In buying and selling he must work assiduously to prevent any shortfall in the revenues of the exalted state.

They (the officers mentioned) must accept him as the appraiser of that place. They must recognize that the duties and customary rights of that position belong to him.

They are to know that there are strict injunctions in this matter.

Notes

1 The terms employed here are *muqīm* (appraiser) and *mihtar* (headman). The latter term seems to refer to the head of a specific lower-ranking occupational group. Cf. Wilson, *Glossary*, p. 338: "Mehtar . . . the head of a caste or business, trade or art, who used to exercise considerable authority over the others." The valuation or appraisal referred to apparently fixed the empire-wide tax on goods, collected at the time of purchase in urban markets. Cf. Ali Muhammad Khan provides a copy of a royal order discussing this form of customs collection in Aurangzeb's reign, p. 284 in *Mirāt-i Aḥmadī*, translated by M. F. Lokhandwala and published by the Oriental Institute (Baroda, 1965).

224b Position of Superintendent of Canals[1]

This order is issued to the responsible officers, workmen, and laborers of the canal located in ______ place: in accordance with the exalted order, the position of superintendent of the aforementioned canal is transferred from ______ and conferred upon ______.

He, (the latter) must fulfill the duties and customary obligations of that
position with rectitude and propriety. As established by custom, he must
properly repair the canal at the time of sowing, with the assistance of the
225a peasants of the villages who use the water of that canal to irrigate their land.
Thus he must ensure an abundant flow of water. He must divide and allocate (the water) in equal shares according to the cultivated area of each of the attached villages so that the populousness and produce of those *maḥals* will increase greatly, resulting in the prosperity of the state and the affluence of the peasants.

They (the officers mentioned) must accept the aforementioned person as superintendent of that place and recognize that the duties and customary rights of that position belong to him.

Notes

1 *See* Habib, *The Agrarian System*, pp. 31–36, for a description of the Mughal irrigation canal system in the north Indian plain, and for the functions of the canal superintendent.

225a Position of Superintendent of the Post (*Ḍākchaukī*)

This order is issued to ______: at this time by the order of Him Who Commands the World, the Resplendent (Emperor), the position of superintendent of the post of ______ province is transferred from ______ and conferred upon that refuge of dignity ______ (the nominee). He must fulfill the duties and customary obligations of that position. He must perform energetically and carefully (his duties) in the required manner. Thus he may ensure the arrival of the post-containers etc. for royal orders without any delay or hindrance.

He must convey, with strict care, the always felicitous imperial edicts and the divine orders issued to the officers of that place. He must despatch to His Resplendent Majesty petitions and news of events and occurrences in conformity with regulation and custom. He must take a bond from the messengers that they will allow nothing extraneous to accompany the containers for written (official) orders. He must ensure that they do not seize or confiscate cesses forbidden by the exalted court, or in any way interfere with travellers and wayfarers.

225b He must report suits in the court of justice, and provide detailed abstracts of the decisions, whether settlements or nonsettlements. He must reveal the particulars, including the condition and number of prisoners held in the fortresses and in the courts (*kachahrī*), and the reasons for their imprisonment.

He must describe (in his reports) the state of affairs of that place succinctly and truthfully, without any deletion or addition.

He should send these (reports) to the Emperor without delay or negligence. He must avoid both excessive partisanship and enmity (in his reporting). What more than this need be decreed?

225b **Position of Superintendent, and Using the Same Content, Collector for the *Maḥals* of Saffron**

This order is issued to the responsible officers, workmen, and laborers of the *maḥals* of saffron of ______ subdistrict located in the province of Kashmir: at this time, the position of superintendent of the aforementioned fiscal units is transferred from ______ and conferred upon ______. In fulfilling the duties and customary obligations of that position with rectitude and propriety, he (the latter) must not permit the slightest matter to escape his vigilance and care. He must be assiduous and vigilant in his work during the season of flowering, picking (of the blossoms) and drying; in setting a price determined by the scarcity or abundance of saffron; increasing the profit for the state; and expanding the trade and sales to the customers.[1]

He must ensure that no one dares to cheat the buyers or adulterate (the saffron), and that the buyers themselves pay the full price of the saffron, leaving absolutely no arrears outstanding.

They (the officers mentioned) must accept him as the superintendent (bearing) absolute (powers). They must recognize that the duties and customary rights of that position belong to him. They are to know that
226a there are strict injunctions in this matter.

Notes

1 Saffron, produced only in Kashmir throughout the Mughal period, was a highly profitable state-controlled export. Cf. Habib, *The Agrarian System*, pp. 73, 75.

226a **Position of Superintendent, and Using the Same Content, the Collector of the Subdistrict Cattle and Slave Market (*Peṅṭh-i Nakhās*)**

This order is issued to the responsible officers, workmen, and staff of the cattle and slave market of ______ city, ______ province: at this time, the position of superintendent of that place is transferred from ______ and conferred upon ______. In fulfilling the duties and customary obligations of that position with rectitude and propriety, he (the latter) must not permit the slightest matter to escape his vigilance and care.

He must take charge of the collections in conformity with established custom and fixed regulations. He must keep himself well informed, to prevent any loss or negligence in all situations or transactions, and to repel any attempted embezzlement or fraud. The Hindu traders must not be able to intermingle their goods with (the goods traded by those) of the Muslim faith. He must take a bond to that effect from the brokers of that place. He must protect and guard the money (held) in the custody of the cashkeeper, so that the cashkeeper is not able to spend a single *dām* without an authentic warrant from the *dīwān*. All the monies in his (the cashkeeper's) charge must be sent to the provincial treasury and a receipt given to the cashkeeper.

They (the officers mentioned) must accept the aforementioned as superintendent of those *maḥals*. They must recognize that the duties and customary rights of that position belong to him.

226a **Position of Land Measurer (or Cadastral Surveyor)[1]**

This order is issued to the responsible officers of the *maḥals* or the royal lands[2]: at this time, the position of land measurer of those *maḥals* is transferred from ______ and conferred upon ______.

In fulfilling the duties and customary obligations of that position with rectitude and propriety, he (the latter) must not permit the slightest matter to escape his vigilance and care. He must send the account papers to the exalted office in conformity with established rules and fixed regulations.

They (the officers mentioned) must accept the aforesaid person as land measurer of those *maḥals*. They must recognize that the duties and customary rights of that position belong to him. They are to know that there are strict injunctions in this matter.

Notes

1 Wilson's *Glossary*, p. 389, translates *paimāna-kash* as a "weighman" or measurer, and associates the term with a number of similar terms referring to land surveying.

2 In *The Agrarian System*, p. 270, Habib describes the *khāliṣa sharīf* "as a group of assignments [*jāgīrs*] held directly by the imperial administration." In other

words, the imperial administration did not necessarily reserve for itself a fixed and bounded territory at the heart of the empire, but instead shifted the crown's possessions among the "most fertile and convenient lands."

226b Bond (*Muchulkā*) for the Position of *Amīn* and *Faujdār*

I am the slave of the court, the Asylum of Mankind. As the *faujdārī* of ______ subdistrict belonging to ______ province has been assigned to the charge of this slave of the court and transferred from ______ by the seat of the *khilāfat* and world-conquering power, I am therefore submitting in writing (that):

I will fulfill the duties and customary obligations of that position with complete rectitude and propriety. I will not permit the slightest matter to escape my vigilance and care.

I will exert every effort to maintain order, to punish malefactors and rebels, to destroy the strongholds of those groups, to protect and succour the subjects and to prevent smiths from manufacturing firearms.

I will order that body (of officers) whom I appoint to the military posts (*thānajāt*) of the *maḥals* of the *faujdārī* (the area under his jurisdiction) not to seize anything in the form of forbidden taxes. No one from that place may use forbidden articles and intoxicating drugs.

If the headmen (*muqaddamān*) from any village (among) the villages (of my jurisdiction) have become unruly and seditious, I shall first seize a number and attempt to reform them by advice and persuasion. They must repent of their stubborn and evil ways, agree to pay the revenue demands, and submit to authority. However, if due to their inherent deceitful villainy they do not reform, I shall attack the aforesaid village and punish the malefactors.

I shall guard the royal roads in such a manner that travellers and wayfarers may move back and forth with composed and tranquil minds. Nowhere will I permit theft or highway robbery. If the property of any person is stolen or plundered I shall return the goods to the owner, and
227a punish that band (of thieves). If I cannot recover (the property), I shall personally reimburse the (rightful) owner for his losses.

I shall not expropriate the tax revenues (*māl*) of the *khāliṣa sharīf* or the *sā'ir.*

I have given these few words in the form of a bond in writing so that thereafter an order (*sanad*) may be issued.[1]

Note

1 As the last sentence in the text suggests, every recipient of an order of appointment, in this case a *sanad*, was required to sign a standard surety form called a bond (*muchulkā*), which put the requirements of the officer either in the first person or used the term the slave of the court (*banda-i dargāh*). A number of these first-person agreement forms survive in the Inayat Jang Collection of the National Archives, New Delhi.

227a Acceptance of the Pledge (*Taahhud*) for the Position of *Amīn* and *Faujdār*[1]

I hereby accept with gratitude and zeal, the position of *amīn* and *faujdār* for ______ subdistrict, ______ district and province for the *maḥals* of *khāliṣa sharīf*, from the beginning of ______ to the end of ______ in accordance with the required one, two, or three year commitment. (I shall) remit the sum of ______ (amount) rupees *sikka mubārak* every year, without intermixing any crude or bad coins of whatever minting. (I shall not collect) anything other than the land revenue (*māl-o-jihāt*) and the proper cesses and allowances.

I affirm that upon confirmation of my appointment, I will convey in each season the stipulated installments of the aforesaid sum to the elevated *sarkār*. I promise that I will deduct the allowance for temporary revenue troops (*sih-bandī*) and for the *zamīndār's* assistance in collection (*nānkār*) etc. according to the scheduled rates for salary assignments (*jāgīrdārī*)[2] and the established custom (*mamūl*).

If, God forbid, some natural calamity should occur, I will notify promptly the officers of the elevated *sarkār*. I shall deduct an allowance (from the stipulated installments) determined by the investigations of the present, trusted *amīn*, (the appointee). If such an extremity should blight the crops, I will sign an authorization for a (further) reduction in my pledged payments, after setting aside (previously) the allowances for *sih-bandī* etc. (as obtained) from the (current) total revenues. (I will calculate) the lost revenues (through crop damage) by setting alongside one another the investigations of the present *amīn*, as well as the original draft (*khām*) registers, the village accountant's (*paṭwārī*) papers, and the signed statements of the subdistrict headmen and accountants. I shall pay the remainder of that pledge to the final *dām*.

I have accordingly written these words of acceptance to serve henceforth as a warrant.[3]

Notes

1 The *ta'ahhud* is defined by Habib as "a pledge given by a prospective official about the amount he would assess or collect." *The Agrarian System*, p. 278. In general, however, as Habib points out, "the difference between the amount of the *ta'ahhud* and the actual revenue collected was not recoverable," i.e. by imperial practice.

2 The meaning of *jāgīrdārī* in this context is not at all certain.

3 The text concludes in the normal fashion, but an additional sentence is appended: "The *kharīf* was four installments; the *rabī* four installments." This phrase could simply refer to the schedule of payments referred to in the text: in the autumn or winter crop season four payments; in the spring season, four payments.

227b Position of Administrator of Surat, the Auspicious Port

At this time, according to the exalted order, the position of administrator (*mutaṣaddī*) of Surat, the Auspicious Port, included within the province of Ahmadabad, the Jewel of Countries is transferred from ______ and conferred upon ______ from the beginning of ______, according to the details specified on the reverse of this document. The recipient must fulfill the duties and customary obligations of that position.

He must (continually) scrutinize all local accounts and affairs, and investigate the demands made by the collectors (*ᶜummāl*). If this examination reveals the collector of a fiscal unit to be dishonest and a wrongdoer, he should report his particulars to His Resplendent Majesty, so that another person may be appointed in his place.

He must exert every effort to punish malefactors and rebels, to destroy the strongholds of that group, to protect and succour the subjects and the local aristocracy, and to prevent smiths from manufacturing firearms. He should order the *thānadārs* (military commanders of fortified posts) whom he appoints to keep order and to seize nothing in the form of forbidden taxes.

No one may indulge in forbidden articles and intoxicants.

If malefactors of any village among those villages have become unruly and seditious, he must seize a number of them. He should then attempt to reform them so that they repent their stubborn and refractory ways, agree to pay their taxes, and submit to authority.

However, if due to their inherent deceitful villainy, these persons do not reform, he may attack that village and punish the malefactors. In so doing he should not molest the smaller cultivators. From any plunder which he may seize, such as livestock, etc. he may confiscate a penalty for the state equal to the proper land revenue demand for the aforesaid village.

He must guard the royal roads so that travellers and wayfarers may move back and forth with composed and tranquil minds. Nowhere may he
228a permit theft and highway robbery. In the event that the property of any person is lost by theft, he must recover those goods when capturing the thieves and highwaymen, and return the goods to their (rightful) owner. He must punish that band of miscreants. If he cannot recover the property, he must reimburse the owner for the value of the aforesaid goods.

He must exert every effort to expand the cultivated area; to resettle the peasants, and promote their welfare and tranquility; and to assess and collect the proper revenues for the royal lands (*khāliṣa sharīf*). He should apportion half (the agricultural produce) to the peasant, and half, without diminution, to the exalted state. He must order the collectors (*karoṛīyān*) to hand over to the treasurer the proceeds of the assessed land revenues. He may collect the additional sum of five rupees per hundred (of the current revenues) against the past years' arrears from the demarcated villages. He must also deposit (those sums) in the treasury. He (the

administrator) must vigilantly protect the revenues of the exalted state from the embezzling grasp of the collectors and treasurers. He must guard the treasury and recover from the cashkeepers and treasurers any amount outstanding from the revenue proceeds. He must remove (these funds) from their charge, have the funds deposited in the general treasury, and have a receipt made out. From the fees allotted to the collectors, he must withhold one rupee per hundred in anticipation of any future audit. He may pay the remainder of the aforesaid fees from the funds collected for arrears and agricultural loans, in accordance with the individual (*sanad*) issued by His Resplendent Majesty. If the aforesaid money is not sufficient to meet the cost of the collectors' allowances, he
228b may pay the necessary amount from the proceeds of the current year. He must collect by the regulation system (*ẓabṭ*) the established revenue proceeds of the ports. He should treat the merchants (of that port) with consideration.

When the harvest season ends he must use the record papers to investigate any embezzlement and fraud by the collectors (*ʿummāl*). He should require them to repay whatever they owe (that appears in their names). He must protect the share (of the revenue) of the holy port of Surat.

The collectors, the *chaudhurīs*, the *qānūngos*, the village headmen, the cultivators, and the peasants of that place must accept the aforementioned person as administrator of that port. They must heed his prudent speech and righteous conduct provided that he attends to the interests of the exalted state and the prosperity of the peasants and rural aristocracy as specified on the reverse of this document. They must attend to his praise or complaint about themselves.

228b

Position of *Dīwān* of the Army

At this time, according to the exalted order, the position of *dīwān* of the army commanded by ______ is conferred upon ______. In fulfilling the duties and customary obligations of that position with rectitude and propriety, he (the latter) must not permit the slightest matter to escape his vigilance and care.

He must collect in the treasury of the army the monies intended for payment of the soldiers' salaries and for other salary headings (accounts) and secure these under his seal. After inspection of (those troops) present (at the muster) he may pay the salaries in conformity with the order of His Resplendent Majesty. And he must not permit the expenditure of a single *dām* without verified authorization from the *dīwān*. Otherwise, he will
229a have to repay and account for such sums.

As required by regulations and custom, he must send the income and expenditure accounts, treasury balances,[1] and other account papers, to the exalted office.

He should conduct himself properly (agreeably) with the clerks, staff,

and salary claimants. He may not tyrannize over his subordinates.

(They) must accept the aforementioned person as *dīwān* of the aforesaid army and recognize that the duties and customary rights of that position belong to him.

Notes

1 The term is *arsaṭh* (also *arsaṭṭā*), cf. John T. Platts, *A Dictionary of Urdu, Classical Hindi, and English* (Oxford, 1930 edition, 1960 reprint), p. 40, a Hindi term meaning primarily cash accounts or a record of daily cash flow.

229a

Position of *Amīn* of *Pāybāqī*[1]

At this time, the position of *amīn* of *pāybāqī* lands, of estates recalled from religious beneficiaries (*a'imma*), and of subsistence lands exempted from taxation (*madad-maʿāsh*) in ______ subdistrict, ______ province, is transferred from ______ and conferred upon ______, according to the (stipulations) of the reverse, from the beginning of ______. He (the recipient) must fulfill the duties and customary obligations of that position with rectitude and propriety. He must treat the peasantry with consideration.

He must bring those *maḥals* (fiscal units, usually subdistricts) recalled into *pāybāqī*, into the regulation system correctly and definitively, that they may provide the salaries of the assignment holders (*jāgīrdārs*). He must assess the value (*jamaʿ*) of those lands after scrutinizing the assessments for past years, made by the agents of previous *jāgīrdārs*, and after informing himself accurately of the existing (economic) conditions. He should then allot half (the produce) to the peasant and half to the exalted state.

He must require the collector (*karoṛī*) to deliver the revenue proceeds into the charge of the treasurer.

If, from time to time, the assessment of any single *maḥal* becomes outdated he must fix that unit's current assessment, and cause the proper revenue to be collected.

Every harvest season he must collect the extra sum of five rupees per hundred rupees of the current assessment from the villages, this additional sum to be applied to clear the outstanding arrears and balance of loans to the peasants. In the first installment of the current year's collections, he should take in that money loaned (*taqāwī*) to the peasants
229b in the previous year.

He must make every effort to expand the cultivated and settled areas.

He must recognize by the fixed rules and his own bond, his personal responsibility for the funds deposited with the treasurer. He (the *amīn*) must repay any amount outstanding in his name from the land revenue or from the stores.

He must ensure that not a single *dām* is spent without an authentic warrant from the *dīwān*. He should despatch all the funds in his charge to the general treasury, providing a receipt to the (local) treasurer. He must take care to reconcile his totals of the revenue collections with the amounts collected by the *jāgīrdār's* agents, leaving not even a single *dām* in arrears. He will be held accountable for any delayed transactions or uncollected arrears.

He must issue a receipt, bearing his seal and the signature of the treasurer, to the peasants for the money they pay the treasury. When all revenue in arrears has been paid in full, he may use those same receipts to compute the total revenue collected.

Save for the proper taxes he must not collect any of the forbidden levies.

He should hold back from the revenue collectors' allowances one rupee (per hundred) against any future audit. He should enter the amount withheld in the revenue assessment (*jama*ᶜ), so that he can explain (account for) that sum in the audit. He may pay the remainder of the aforesaid allowance to the collectors in conformity with each one's individual order (*sanad*), from the collected revenue arrears and loan repayments. If the aforementioned money is not sufficient to pay the collectors' allowances, he may pay the additional amount from the collections of the current year.

He must send the account papers to the exalted office according to regulations.

The *chaudhurīs* and *qānūngos*, the village headmen, the cultivators, and the peasants of that place must accept that position as belonging to the
230a aforementioned person. They must recognise his contract (*qaul-o-qarār*), assessments (*tashkhīs*), and authority as approved and valid. They must heed his prudent speech and righteous conduct. And they must attend to his praise or blame about themselves.

Notes

1 *Pāybāqī* lands were those villages or subdistricts administered temporarily by agents of the central administration pending reassignment to pay the salaries of other Mughal officers (*manṣabdārs*). Cf. Habib, *The Agrarian System*, p. 259n.

230a Position of Revenue Collector (*Karoṛī*) of *Pāybāqī Maḥals*, of Estates Recalled from Religious Beneficiaries (*A'imma*) and Tax-exempt Land Grants (*Madad-Ma*ᶜ*āsh*)

The position of revenue collector for *maḥals* of *pāybāqī*, for estates recalled from religious beneficiaries, and for the lands (partially) exempted from taxation in ______ subdistrict, ______ district and province, in conformity with the details specified upon the reverse of this document, is conferred upon ______ from the beginning of ______. He must fulfill the

duties and customary obligations of that position with rectitude and propriety. He must treat the peasantry with consideration.

He must bring those *maḥals* recalled into *pāybāqī*, into the regulation system, to provide the correct and definitive salaries of assignment holders. He (the *karoṛī*) must collect the fixed and proper total revenue that the *amīn*, with his advice, has assessed. (The *amīn's* determination is based upon) careful scrutiny of the revenue demanded in past years by agents of previous *jāgīrdārs*, and full knowledge of existing conditions. He must deliver whatever he collects to the treasurer. If any *maḥal* has not yet been assessed, he may make collections from that (unit) upon the advice of the *amīn*.

Every harvest season he must collect an extra five rupees per hundred of the current revenue demand for the villages, this additional sum to be applied against any arrears and balances of loans to the peasants. In the current year's first collections, he should include that money loaned to the peasants in the previous year. He must take great care to reconcile these (his returns) with those of the agents of the *jāgīrdārs*, leaving not a single
230b *dām* in arrears. He will be held accountable for any delayed transactions and remaining arrears. He must issue a receipt, bearing his seal and the signature of the treasurer, for the money that the peasants pay to the treasury. When the revenue collections in arrears have been paid in full, he may use those same receipts to compute the total revenue collected.

He must collect only the proper taxes, and not any forbidden levies.

He should hold back from his revenue collection allowance one rupee per hundred against any future audit. He should enter this in the revenue assessment (*jama*^{c}) so that he can explain (account for) that sum during the audit. He may take the remainder of the aforesaid allowance, in conformity with his individual order (*sanad*) and with the approval of the *amīn*, from the collected arrears and loan repayments. If the aforementioned money is not sufficient to pay the collector's allowance, he may take the necessary amount from the collections of the current year.

He must send the account papers to the exalted office according to regulations.

The *chaudhurīs* and *qānūngos*, the village headmen, the cultivators, and the peasants of that place must recognize the aforementioned person as the collector of those *maḥals*, and the duties and customary rights of that position as belonging to him.

230b **Order for the Position of Abolisher of Forbidden Beliefs (*Raf*^{c}*-i Abwāb-i Mamnū*^{c})**[1]

The responsible officers of the Jewel of Countries, Ahmadabad Province, are hereby informed: at this time, according to the exalted order, the position of abolisher of forbidden beliefs, attached to the aforesaid province, is transferred from ______ and conferred upon ______. He (the

appointee) must fulfill the duties and customary obligations of that position with rectitude and propriety. He must not permit the slightest matter to escape his vigilance and care. He must act as strictly as is necessary to abolish forbidden beliefs, according to the commandments
231a of the resplendent Holy Law. He should appoint an orthodox prayer leader (*imām*) and an orthodox caller to prayer (*mu'azzin*) for the *masjid* built by the *Ismāʿīlī* sect (*qaum*). He must see that forbidden articles and intoxicating liquors are not used. He must take a bond from that sect (*farīq*) that they now repudiate the deranged claims of those people (the *Ismāʿīlī* leaders).

The aforesaid position is hereby conferred upon the aforementioned person. The duties and customary rights of that position belong to him. They are to know that there are strict injunctions in this matter.

Notes

1 This particular office reflects the Emperor Aurangzeb's continuing effort to stamp out *Ismāʿīlī* activities in Gujarat. The compiler of the *Mir'āt-i Aḥmadī* reported that the Emperor summoned Sayyid Shahji, a wealthy and popular *Ismāʿīlī* spiritual leader living in Ahmadabad, to the imperial court *circa* 1100 A.H./A.D. 1688–89. The subsequent death of the Sayyid by suicide touched off a massive series of revolts by his followers. The Governor of Ahmadabad Province suppressed these only with much effort and bloodshed. Thereafter imperial officers continued to press the members of this sect very hard to abandon their unorthodox beliefs and allegiance for the remainder of Aurangzeb's reign. See Ali Muhammad Khan, *Mir'āt-i Aḥmadī*, pp. 286–289, and Aniruddha Ray, "Francis Martin's Account of the Rising of the Matiyas in 1685," in *Proceedings of the Indian History Congress* (1969): 195–203.

231a Charge-Order (*Sanad-i Sipurd*) to Defray the Expenses of Special Robes of Honor[1] (*Malbūs-i khāṣṣ*)

At this time, according to the exalted order, the sum of ______ (amount) *dāms* (assessed revenue) from ______ subdistrict, ______ district and province, which upon the transfer of ______ has been recalled into the temporary pool of lands awaiting assignment (*pāybāqī*) in the *khāliṣa sharīf*. From the beginning of ______ this (revenue) has been placed in the charge[2] of that most noble person to defray expenses for special robes of honor (*malbūs-i khāṣṣ*). He must make a strenuous effort to increase the population, to extend the cultivated area, to expand the revenue collections of the exalted state, and to preserve the tranquility of the peasantry.

Having acquired this allowance from the revenue proceeds, he must prepare the special robes of honor in conformity with the requirements of the purchasing establishment (*ibtiyāʿkhāna*). He must send them (the robes) to His Resplendent Majesty. They are to know that there are strict injunctions in this matter.

Notes

1 Cf. M. Athar Ali, *Mughal Nobility*, p. 140, for the term *malbūs-khāṣṣ*. The *k͟hilʿats* or robes of honor were highly decorated dresses, girdles, and caps made of from three to seven separate pieces. The Emperor was usually the first person to wear these special robes, whether symbolically or actually, and he then presented them personally to the recipient. This presentation created a ritual bond between the Mughal throne and the *manṣabdār* who received the robes.

2 This phrase might also have a more technical meaning; the term translated as 'charge' is *ʿuhda*, meaning an obligation or responsibility, and a variant of *taʿahhud*, the pledge of the revenue collector (see folio 227a). Thus this officer may have had to collect all revenues from this territory as well as these special revenues.

231a Position of Highway Patrol Commander (*Rāhdār*) and Military Commander of a Fortified Post (*Thānadār*)

At this time the position of highway patrol commander, and fortified post command for ______ place included within ______ province is transferred from ______ and conferred upon ______ in conformity with the details specified on the reverse of this document. He (the appointee) must fulfill the duties and customary obligations of that position with rectitude and propriety. He must exert every effort to maintain order, to administer according to the regulations, to punish and chastise malefactors and rebels, to protect and succour both the smaller cultivators and larger taxpayers, and to prevent smiths from manufacturing firearms. He must take special care that no one uses forbidden articles or intoxicating drugs.
231b He must guard the royal roads so that travellers and wayfarers may move back and forth with composed and tranquil minds. He must eliminate all trace of thieves or highway robbers. If the property of any person is stolen or plundered, he must recover it when capturing the thieves and highwaymen, and return the goods to their (rightful) owner. He must punish that band of miscreants. If he cannot recover the property he must reimburse the owner for (the value of) the aforesaid goods.

The *chaudhurīs* and *qānūngos*, the *zamīndārs*, village headman, cultivators, and peasants of that place must accept the charge of highway patrol commander and post commander for that locality as conferred upon the aforementioned person. They must recognize that the duties and customary rights of that position belong to him.

231b Position of the *Īrmān* (Ruler) of the *Tūmān* (District) of *Peshāwar*

The responsible officers and regulators of affairs, present and future, the chiefs (*malikān*), headmen (*muqaddamān*), cultivators, and peasants of the *tūmān* of Peshāwar included within the *Dār al-mulk* Kābul are hereby

informed: at this time, according to the exalted order, the position of *Īrmān* of the district of Peshāwar is transferred from ______ and conferred upon ______ in conformity with the details set out on the reverse of this document.

He (the recipient) must fulfill the duties and customary obligations of that (position) with rectitude and propriety. He must not permit the slightest matter to escape his vigilance and care.

He must do his utmost to administer correctly the revenues of that aforementioned district, and to safeguard the tranquility of the peasantry on the frontier (*marzbūm*). He must rely on no other person as his partner or associate.

Every year, he must deposit in the treasury of the aforesaid province (Kābul), an installment of five thousand rupees, toward a total of forty thousand rupees *peshkash* (tribute) for the exalted state, (to be paid in full) within eight years.

He may take the chief's allowances and the tax-exempt lands of the *Īrmān* (belonging to) his grandfather and father, but he must not desire or expect more than this.

The aforesaid position is conferred upon the aforementioned person and they (the officers) must recognize that the duties and customary
232a rights of that position belong to him. They must apportion the tax-exempt land grants, perquisites, *zamīndārs'* revenue collection allowances (*nānkār*), expenses for the royal table (*kharj alūshī*), revenue assessment, etc., of Peshāwar, in consultation with him.[1] They are to know that there are strict injunctions in this matter.

Notes

1 This listing of categories of allowances and revenues is extremely confused. Qureshi, in *The Administration of the Mughal Empire*, p. 237, cites the *Ā'īn-i Akbarī* of Abul Fazl for the basic administrative unit in Kabul province as a *tūmān*. From the time of Chingiz Khan, and before, the Mongols had utilized the decimal principle of army organization in which the largest single unit was the *tūmān* or 10,000 horsemen.

232a Position of Superintendent of the *Dīwān*'s Office and Establishment (*Dārogha-i Kachahrī*)

This order is issued to the responsible officers, functionaries, and staff of the *dīwān's* office (*kachahrī*) of ______ province: at this time, according to the exalted order, the position of superintendent of the aforementioned *kachaharī* is transferred from ______ and conferred upon ______. He (the appointee) must fulfill the duties and customary obligations of that position with rectitude and propriety. He must not allow the slightest matter to escape his vigilance and care. He must take care to prevent any loss or negligence in all transactions and affairs of that place.

He must prepare accurate copies of the account papers from the

subdistricts (*parganāt*). After the provincial *dīwān* has scrutinized the accounts, the superintendent must ensure that they are sent each year to the sublime office (at the imperial capital). He (the superintendent), using extreme care, may collect and deposit in the provincial treasury (*khizāna-i ʿāmira*) any officer's outstanding balance as established by treasury claims and accounts,[1] and certified by the provincial *dīwān*.

They (the officers mentioned) must accept the aforementioned person as *dārogha-i kachahrī*. They must recognize that the duties and customary rights of that position belong to him.

Notes

1 "*Muṭālaba wa muḥāsaba bāshad*" refers to the financial transactions ongoing between each imperial officer (*manṣabdār*) and the various imperial treasuries. Mughal officers often took treasury loans or advances against their salaries, or incurred fines for various infractions of regulations, and thus acquired fiscal obligations to the treasury. On the other hand, delayed salary payments or *jāgīr* assignments gave them a claim against the treasury. These various account balances were sorted out at periodic intervals, as well as at the death or retirement of the officer. For a more detailed explanation, *see* M. Athar Ali, *The Mughal Nobility*, pp. 51–53.

232a **Position of Superintendent of Grain Sales (*Dārogha-i Mubīʿi Ghallāt*)**

This order is issued to the responsible officers, clerks, and staff of ______ (place): at this time, the position of superintendent of grain sales is transferred from ______ and conferred upon ______. He (the appointee) must fulfill the duties and customary obligations of that position with
232b rectitude and propriety.

He should time the sale of grain to produce the maximum profit. He must deposit the money realized from that (sale) in charge of the cashkeeper (treasurer). He must not expand a single *dām* from (the funds under) his charge without an authentic warrant from the *dīwān*. He must have all the funds in his charge sent to the provincial treasury, from which he must obtain a receipt.

They (the officers mentioned) must accept the aforementioned person as superintendent of grain sales for that place and recognize that the duties and customary rights of that position belong to him.

232b **Position of Claims Settlement Officer (*Istīfā'*)**

This order is issued to ______: at this time, the position of claims settlement officer of ______ is transferred from ______ and conferred upon him. He must fulfill all the duties and customary obligations of that position with rectitude and propriety. He must not let the slightest point of information escape him in examining the final accounts and the

treasury claims. Having computed and settled the accounts according to the regulations, he must bring them to the *dīwān* of the province for his signature. Thereafter, in accordance with that (computation), he may exact the necessary deductions and demand restitution. They (the officers of that place) are to know that there are strict injunctions in this matter.

232b Position of Secretary (*Peshkār*) to the *Dīwān* of the Army

This order is issued to the responsible officers, the clerks and staff of the *dīwān* of the army under the command of (*hamrāhī*) ______: at this time the position of secretary for the *dīwān* of the aforementioned army is conferred upon ______. He must fulfill the duties and customary obligations of that position with rectitude and propriety. He must not permit the slightest matter to escape his vigilance and care. He must be careful not to permit a single *dām* to be paid (to the army) from the money allocated for salaries (*tankhwāh*) or other types of claims in the army treasury, without an authentic warrant from the *dīwān* of the army.
233a He must scrutinize minutely all salary payments, recognizing his obligation under the regulations to investigate these (transactions) thoroughly.

In conformity with regulations, he must prepare corrected and detailed copies for the *dīwān* of the income and expense records, treasury balances, and other account papers and have these sent to the exalted office (at the imperial capital or camp).

Having treated the clerks and staff with consideration, he must carry out his tasks with integrity. They must recognize that the aforementioned position is conferred upon the aforesaid person and that the duties and customary rights of that position belong to him.

233a Position of Superintendent and Assessor of *Sā'ir*

This is issued to the responsible officers, clerks, and staff of the *maḥals* of *sā'ir* of ______ province: at this time in accordance with the exalted order, the position of superintendent (*dārogha*) (or) assessor (*amīn*) of the aforementioned *maḥals* is transferred from ______ and conferred upon ______. He (the appointee) must fulfill the duties and customary obligations of that position with rectitude and propriety. He must not allow the slightest matter to escape his vigilance and care.

He should take in the proceeds of the two and one-half and five per cent[1] tax according to the established rules and deposit them with the treasurer. He should regard the protection and guarding of the funds in his (the treasurer's) custody as a personal obligation. He must not permit a single *dām* to be expended without an authentic warrant from the *dīwān*. He (the *amīn*) must be sure that all the funds in his custody arrive at the general treasury and that he obtains a full receipt. At night he must guard

the merchants' goods under his own seal and that of the superintendent (*dārogha*). He must repay from his allowance, according to the fixed rules, each *dām* from the proceeds of goods (sold) there that he may
233b deduct or divert for his own use. He must be extremely careful to prevent the Hindu traders from certifying their own goods under the names of Muslims. He should take a bond to that effect from the brokers of that place.

They (the officers mentioned above) must accept the aforementioned person as either the superintendent or the *amīn* of that place. They must recognize that the duties and customary rights of that position belong to him.

Notes

1 The Emperor Aurangzeb reimposed the canonical Islamic tax levied on the import and export of commodities in the twenty-fifth year of his reign. Muslim traders, as stated above, paid two and one-half per cent on value for commodities at the time and place of the original purchase. Hindus paid five per cent at the time of purchase, and Christians and Jews paid three and one-half per cent. *See* Qureshi, *The Administration of the Mughal Empire*, pp. 146–147, for a discussion of this practice.

233b In the Order (*Sanad*) for the Position of Collector of the Treasury[1]

This additional statement must be written: That he must vigilantly guard and patrol (*gird-awārī*) the transfer (importation) of monies from the stations, customs houses, and outlying areas, so that the flow of such funds may not be interrupted.

Notes

1 This section is apparently an addition for the letter given to a new treasury collector. See folio 237a below.

233b Falconry Order (*Dastak-ī Qūshkhāna*)

This order is issued in the names of the agents of the *faujdārs*, *jāgīrdārs*, customs officers (*guzarbānān*), and officers protecting the roads and highways: a document bearing the seal of the falconry officers of the exalted state (the Emperor) has arrived at the central office. (The document states) that those creatures (the falcons) under the care of ______, head falconers, have gone for moulting to ______ subdistrict. His Resplendent Majesty has ordered that: customs dues and road taxes must be set aside in every place where those officers may cause those hunting animals to alight. They (the local officers) must supply whatever may be demanded for (the falcons') food, such as small birds and minced meat, etc., without delay, or they may provide an allowance (of money) equivalent to the prevailing price of those (supplies).

Thus (the imperial officers) must take care that no one uses threats or force to make them (the falcons) alight at the residence of anyone. No assailant may harm or injure those creatures.

233b **Position of Assayer (*Chaukasī*) and Master Weigher (*Wazn-kash*) of the Mint**

234a This order is issued to the responsible officers, clerks and staff of the mint of ______ place: at this time the position of assayer and master weigher for gold and silver of the aforementioned *maḥals* is transferred from ______ and conferred upon ______. He (the appointee) must fulfill the duties and obligations of that position with rectitude and propriety. He must not permit the slightest matter to escape his vigilance and care.

He must try to satisfy the traders (*baipārīyān*) (who deal with the mint) completely and to create abundant proceeds for the exalted state. He must ensure that the *ashrafī* (gold coins) and rupees (silver coins) arrive at the required weight and the finest assay in conformity with the rules for the coin of current issue (*sikka mubārak*). According to practice, he may take eight *annas* for every one thousand rupees (struck) as his allowance (for the master weigher and assayer), but apart from that, he may demand nothing more.

They (the officers mentioned) must accept the aforementioned person as assayer and master weigher of the aforesaid *maḥals* and they must recognize that the duties and customary rights of that position belong to him.

234a **Position of Writer of Receipts for *Manṣabdārs* (*Qabẓ-nawīsī Manṣabdārān*)**

This order is issued to the responsible officers, clerks, and staff of the provincial treasury: at this time, the position of writer of receipts for the *manṣabdārs* of that place is transferred from ______ and conferred upon ______. He (the appointee) must completely fulfill the duties and customary obligations of that position. He must not allow the slightest matter to escape his care and vigilance.

He must send the *manṣabdārs'* receipts to the exalted office according to regulations.

They (the officers mentioned) must accept the aforementioned person as writer of receipts for the *manṣabdārs* of that place. They must recognize that the duties and customary rights of that position belong to him.

234a **Position of *Amīn* for Payment of Stipends to Daily Pensioners, etc.**

234b This order is issued to the officers of the *sā'ir maḥals* of the Royal Grain Market and the Market of the Stirrup, etc., located within the royal capital at Delhi, and with the Stirrup of Felicity (the imperial camp): at this time the position of *amīn* for payment of cash stipends to the daily, monthly, and yearly pensioners of that place is transferred from ______ and conferred upon ______. He must fulfill the duties and customary obligations of that (position) with rectitude and propriety. He must not allow the slightest matter to escape his vigilance and care.

He should draw the funds for the stipends of that group from the officers of the aforesaid *maḥals*. He may make cash payments (to the pensioners) after verifying the authenticity of the grants, the sanctity of their persons, and the presence of the provincial *dīwān's* seal on their payment orders in accordance with regulations. He (the *amīn*) must obtain a receipt bearing the seal of each recipient. He (the *amīn*) must despatch, for each year, the (accounts of) total expenditures for that (purpose) to the exalted office.

They (the above mentioned officers) must accept the aforementioned *khān* as *amīn* for payment of cash stipends. They must recognize that the duties and customary right of that (position) belong to him.

234b **Master of the Docks and Superintendent of the Salt Works of the Port**

This order is issued to the responsible officers of Surat, the Auspicious Port, included within the province of Ahmadabad: at this time, according to the exalted order, the position of master of the docks and superintendent of the salt works of the aforementioned port is transferred from ______ and conferred upon ______. He (the appointee) must fulfill the duties and customary obligations of that position with rectitude and propriety. He must not permit the slightest matter to escape his vigilance
235a and care. He must treat the merchants, etc., with consideration.

He must take all necessary precautions in collecting the revenues of the exalted state. He should also take care to prevent any omission or neglect in the affairs of that place.

They (the officers mentioned) must accept the aforementioned as master of the docks and superintendent of the salt works of that place. They must recognize that the duties and customary rights of that position belong to him.

235a **Position of Harbor Master and Superintendent of Boats (*Mīr-baḥrī wa Dārogha-i Nawāra*)[1]**

This order is issued to the responsible officers, clerks, and staff under the harbor master of ______ place: at this time, according to the exalted

order, the position of harbor master of that place is transferred from ______ and conferred upon ______. He must fulfill the duties and customary obligations of that position with rectitude and propriety. He must not allow the slightest matter to escape his vigilance and concern.

He must protect the ships (*kashtīhā*) carefully at nightfall. He must use the utmost vigilance to ensure that none of the malefactors and rebels are able (to board the ships) and cross over.

They must accept the aformentioned person as harbor master of that place. They must recognize that the duties and customary rights of that position belong to him.

Notes

1 Cf. I. H. Qureshi, *The Administration of the Mughal Empire*, p. 231: "The provincial *mīr baḥr* was responsible for the maintenance of the river and sea ports within his jurisdiction in good condition, to guard and supervise river communications and to keep the *nawwārah* in good order." The Mughals used the term *nawāra* for the various imperial fleets employed for military and patrolling purposes in Bengal and other coastal provinces. These fleets were composed of both riverine and coastal craft, equipped with both oars and sails. The *mir baḥrī* could also, depending upon the context, be a high-ranking officer placed in charge of a war fleet. This role was especially critical in the long-drawn-out Mughal expansion into Bengal between A.D. 1570 and 1670. *See* Atul Chandra Roy, *A History of Mughal Navy and Naval Warfares* (Calcutta, 1972), for a detailed treatment of Mughal naval organization, ships and boats, and administration.

235a Position of *Amīn* of the City Magistrate's Office

This order is issued to the responsible officers, clerks, and staff of the magistrate's office of ______ city: according to the exalted order, the position of *amīn* of the office of the aforesaid magistrate is transferred from ______ and conferred upon ______. He (the appointee) must fulfill the duties and customary obligations of that position with rectitude and propriety. He should not permit the slightest matter to escape his vigilance and care. He should conduct himself properly with the clerks and staff of that place. He must take special care to prevent any omission
235b or neglect in the affairs of that place. They must accept the aforementioned as *amīn* of that place and recognize that the duties and customary rights of that (position) belong to him.

235b Position of Secretary (*Peshkār*) to the *Dīwān* of the Province

This order is issued to the responsible officers, clerks and staff of the *dīwān's* office of ______ province: according to the exalted order, the position of secretary of the *dīwān's* office of the aforesaid province, is transferred from ______ and conferred upon ______. He must fulfill the

duties and customary obligations of that position with rectitude and propriety. He must not allow the slightest matter to escape his vigilance and care. He is to prepare the account papers for the *dīwān's* office of the aforesaid province according to regulations. He must despatch the *dīwān's* copies, the salary claim papers, etc., for each year to the central office in conformity with the fixed rules. He must take great care to prevent any omission or neglect in transacting the affairs of that place.

They must accept that aforementioned person as secretary to the *dīwān's* office of the aforesaid province. And they must recognize that the duties and customary rights of that (position) belong to him.

235b Position of Supervisor and Captain of Ships (*Nākhudā*) for the Port of Surat

This order is issued to the responsible officers and those entrusted with the management of affairs, the clerks and staff of the Port of Holy Surat, the Jewel of Countries, Ahmadabad province: at this time, according to the exalted order, the position of supervisor and captain of ships for the exalted state, assigned to the aforesaid port, is transferred from ______ and conferred upon ______ in conformity with the details set out on the reverse of this document. He (the appointee) must attend to the duties and customary obligations of that position with rectitude and propriety, reliably and honestly. He must not permit the slightest matter to escape
236a his vigilance and care. He must conduct himself properly with the clerks and staff of that place.

The aforementioned positions having been assigned to the charge of the aforesaid person, they (the officers mentioned) must recognize that the duties and customary rights of that position belong to him. Moreover, they must follow his orders in executing the business of that place.

236a Position of Superintendent (*Dārogha*) of the Treasury

This order is issued to the responsible officers, clerks and staff of the treasury of ______ province: at this time, according to the exalted order, the position of superintendent of the aforesaid treasury is transferred from ______ and conferred upon ______. He (the appointee) must fulfill the duties and customary obligations of that position with rectitude and propriety. He must not permit the slightest matter to escape his vigilance and care.

Having truly protected the treasury, he must inform himself fully so as to prevent any discrepancy between payments and withdrawals. He must not expend a single *dām* without an authentic certificate from the *dīwān*. He should secure the accumulated money in the vault of the treasury, and then lock the vault and seal it with his seal and that of the treasurer. Only in his own (the superintendent's) presence may it (the vault) be opened or

closed. He must be extremely careful to repel any attempt at embezzlement.

They (the officers mentioned) must accept the aforementioned person as superintendent of the aforesaid treasury. And they must recognize that the duties and customary rights of that position belong to him.

236a **Position of Headman (*Chaudhurī*) of the Money Changers' Market (*Ṣarrāfa*)[1]**

This order is issued to the responsible officers, clerks, and staff of the money changers' market of ______ city: at this time, the position of headman of the money changers' market of the aforesaid city is transferred from ______ and conferred upon ______. He (the appointee) must
236b fulfill the duties and customary obligations of this position with rectitude and propriety. He must not permit the slightest matter to escape his vigilance and care.

He must send to the officers of that place a memorandum of the best market purchase price for silver coin.

He should gratify the clerks and staff of that place by his proper conduct. He should not demand from the money changers (*ṣarrāfān*) anything other than his established customary dues, and he should not introduce new or forbidden exactions.

They must accept the aforementioned person as headman of the money changers' market of the aforesaid city. And they must recognize that the duties and customary rights of that belong to him. They may not exceed the bounds of prudent speech, appropriate behavior and righteous conduct with him while he is attending to the prosperity of the exalted state and the tranquillity of the populace.

Notes

1 The *ṣarrāf*, here translated as money changer, played an indispensable role in the economy of Mughal India. Usually Hindu and members of a regional trading caste, the *ṣarrāfs* (English corruption 'shroff') provided a money-changing service for all comers. They accepted Manila dollars, South Indian gold *hūn* (pagodas), or any of dozens of foreign and indigenous coins in exchange for equivalent Mughal rupees, current issue acceptable at official treasuries, or for any other desired currency. The exchange rate was determined by prevailing market conditions, the condition of the proferred coins, and by the small service charge made by the money changer. *Ṣarrāfs* also took coin and bullion to the Mughal provincial mint and paid to have this melted and struck in silver or gold currency which they returned to circulation. In return for a small discount the *ṣarrāfs* offered bills of exchange (*huṇḍī*), usually payable within two months to the bearer, and saleable. These could be used to despatch money from one city or town to another. The exchange or *ṣarrāfat* of money changers organized in one urban center balanced off accounts with other collectivities of *ṣarrāfs* in order to operate this system. Finally, the *ṣarrāfs* offered credit for commerce, for administration or

any other purposes, either by straight loans or by use of *huṇḍīs.* For an enlarged description of the role of the *ṣarrāf, see* Irfan Habib, "Banking in Medieval India," in Tapan Raychaudhuri, ed., *Contributions to Indian Economic History*, 1 (1960): 8–14, and "Usury in Medieval India," *Comparative Studies in Society and History* (1964): 393–419. Habib has revised some of his earlier views in an essay on "The System of Bills of Exchange (Hundīs) in the Mughal Empire," in *Proceedings of the Indian History Congress* (1972): 209–303.

236b **Position of Accountant (*Mushrif*) of a Subdistrict**

This order is issued to the responsible officers of ______ subdistrict (*pargana*), of ______ district and ______ province: at this time the position of accountant of the aforesaid subdistrict is transferred from ______ and conferred upon ______. He (the appointee) must fulfill the duties and customary obligations of that position with rectitude and propriety. He must not permit the slightest matter to escape his vigilance and care.

He must prepare the account papers of that place in conformity with fixed regulations and established rules so that any future investigation (or audit) will not reveal any discrepancy or surplus. He must despatch (those records) to the exalted office (the office of the provincial *dīwān*).

He must not pay a salary to anyone from the funds in charge of the cashkeeper of that place without an authentic warrant from the *dīwān*. If (he does) so, he will be personally responsible (to answer for that sum).

He must conduct himself properly so as to gratify the clerks and staff and he must display the utmost integrity in fulfilling the requirements of
237a this position. They must accept the aforementiond person as accountant of that place. They must recognize that the duties and customary rights of that position belong to him.

237a **Collector for the Treasury and Transmittal Officer (*Sazāwal*) for Cash Installments of the *Pargana***

This order is issued in the names of the responsible officers, clerks, and staff of ______ subdistrict, and ______ district and ______ province: at this time, the position of collector and transmittal officer for cash installments of the aforesaid subdistrict is transferred from ______ and conferred upon ______. He (the appointee) must fulfill the duties and customary obligations of this position with rectitude and propriety. He must not permit the slightest matter to escape his vigilance and care. He must protect the treasury so as to avoid any discrepancy between income and expenditure. He must not allow a single *dām* or *dirham* to be spent without an authentic warrant from the *dīwān*. He must send, without any delay, the cash installments of the subdistrict to His Resplendent Majesty.

They (the officers mentioned) must accept the aforementioned person as collector of the treasury and transmittal officer for the cash installments of the aforesaid subdistrict. They must recognize that the duties and customary rights of this position belong to him.

237a Position of News Writer (*Akhbār-nawīs*) for the Subdistrict

This order is issued to ______: at this time the position of news writer of ______ subdistrict is transferred from ______ and conferred upon ______. He (the appointee) must fulfill the duties and customary obligations of that (position) with complete rectitude and propriety. He must not permit the slightest matter to escape his vigilance and care.

He must inform himself of the transactions and events of the aforesaid subdistrict in detail, with complete profundity and accuracy. He must prepare copies of the news reports free of any discrepancy, abridgement, or
237b deletion. He must prepare them so as to prevent any omission or neglect. He must send these copies to His Resplendent Majesty. He is to know that there are strict injunctions in this matter.

237b Position of Superintendent (*Dārogha*) of the Treasury and Transmittal Officer (*Sazāwal*) for Provincial Records

This order is issued to the responsible officer of ______ province: at this time, according to the exalted order, the position of superintendent of the treasury and transmittal officer for provincial records for the aforesaid province, is transferred from ______ and conferred upon ______. He (the appointee) must fulfill the duties and customary obligations of that (position) with rectitude and propriety. He must not allow the slightest matter to escape his vigilance and care. In accordance with fixed regulations and established rules, and in cooperation with the *dīwān* of the province and the *amīn* (of the treasury), he must deposit in the treasury the accumulated revenue proceeds of the subdistricts, treasury claims against *jāgīrdārs* (*muṯālabāt*), and other taxes and cesses (taxes other than revenue). He is to lock the door of the treasury and secure it with his own seal. It must be opened and closed (only) in his presence.

He must take special care to repel any attempt at embezzlement or fraud. He may expend nothing without an authentic warrant from the *dīwān*.

Every fifteen days in conformity with the rules, he must send to His Resplendent Majesty the account papers showing the treasury balances. He must ensure that the revenue collectors of the reserved lands of that province (*ʿummāl-ī maḥāl-ī khāliṣa sharīf*) prepare the current revenue assessment (*daul-jamaʿ*), the summary of revenue proceeds and arrears (*wāṣilbāqī*), and other account papers according to fixed regulations and established rules. He should send these (records first for) scrutiny to the

provincial *dīwān*, and thereafter to the central office without delay or procrastination.

They (the officers mentioned) must accept the aforementioned person as superintendent of the treasury and transmittal officer for provincial records of that place, in conformity with the imperial mandate (*yarlīgh*).

237b 238a

Position of Record Keeper (*Mushrif*) of the Magistrate's Gaol (*Paṇḍit-khāna Chabūtara*)

This order is issued to the responsible officers, clerks, and staff, of the magistrate's office of the Stirrup of Felicity (the imperial camp) or to the capital, *Dār al-khilāfat, Shāhjahānābād* (Delhi): at this time, the position of recond keeper for the gaol of the aforesaid establishment is transferred from ______ and conferred upon ______. He (the appointee) must fulfill completely the duties and customary obligations of this position. He must not permit the slightest matter to escape his vigilance and care.

In conformity with regulations, he must maintain the official records showing for each prisoner the cause of imprisonment and the reason for discharge.

They (the officers mentioned) must accept him as record keeper of the gaol and recognize that the duties and customary rights of that position belong to him.

238a

Position of Head Mace-Bearer (*Mīr-dah*) (or) Head Staff-Bearer (*Danḍī*) (or) Head Bailiff (*Nāẓir*)[1]

This order is issued to the responsible officers, clerks and staff of ______ (place): at this time the position of head mace-bearer, head staff-bearer, or head bailiff of that place is transferred from ______ and conferred upon ______. He (the appointee) must fulfill the duties and customary obligations (of that position) with rectitude and propriety. He must not permit the slightest matter to escape his vigilance and care.

He must ensure that the footmen assigned to that place are on duty and fully attentive in the royal work.

They must accept the aforementioned person as head mace-bearer, head staff-bearer, or head bailiff of that place. They must recognize that the duties and customary rights of that position belong to him.

Notes

1 All three terms referred to the commanders of small bodies of armed footmen used by the imperial administration as guards and attendants at various public audiences, for the law courts, etc. These men were not really soldiers nor utilized as such. They also carried important messages and summons for the higher-ranking provincial officers. The appearance of mace-bearers sent directly from the Emperor at the camp or office of a provincial governor or other officer was a notable, but frequently ominous, occasion for the recipient. The

imperial mace-bearers, wearing brocaded robes and carrying either gold or silver maces, were supposed to be received as directly representing the Emperor's person. However, apparently less awesome mace-bearers served in more mundane capacities under provincial governors and *dīwāns*. In A.D. 1694, for example, a rebellious *zamīndār* captured a mace-bearer carrying cash for the treasury of Ganjikota fort in Hyderabad province. The *zamīndār* held the mace-bearer for ransom for two months. Cf. Richards, *Mughal Administration in Golconda*, pp. 119–120.

238a According to the Exalted Order in the Name of the Governor of Bengal Province (after writing the titles)

At this time, ______, etc., bankers (*sāhūān*), in conformity with the standing order, have placed the sum of ______ *lakh* (amount, in hundreds of thousands of rupees) in the general treasury of the Stirrup of Felicity (the Emperor's court or camp).[1] As compensation for this aforesaid amount, of ______ (amount) rupees, and for the expense for discount on a bill of exchange (*hunḍāwan*)[2] and gratuities (*inᶜām*) fixed at three months, payment has been ordered from the treasury of the Paradise of
238b Countries, Bengal. Therefore according to the sublime elevated order, let the person holding the dignity of authority and governance make this payment speedily when he has received the order (*parwāna*) from His Resplendent Majesty issued in the name of the *dīwān* of the province. They are to know that the Refuge of Mankind (the Emperor) has imposed strict injunctions in this matter.

Notes

1 This standard order was probably used for the transfer of the surplus revenues from Bengal to the central treasury. From A.D. 1700 on, after Murshid Qulī Khān was assigned to Bengal as provincial *dīwān* and had reorganized the provincial administration, the Bengal surplus became the financial mainstay of the Emperor Aurangzeb and his immediate successors. By A.D. 1702 Murshid Qulī Khān was sending an annual sum of ten million silver rupees to the Emperor – an extraordinary amount in view of the rural unrest and therefore plummeting revenues elsewhere in the Mughal empire at this time. Murshid Qulī Khān continued to remit enormous sums to the centre from Bengal until his death in A.D. 1727. However, this order does reveal one apparent discrepancy with what is known of the usual mode of remittance. The cost of bills of exchange would have been prohibitive, even if possible, for such large sums, and the *dīwān* therefore had the treasure, in silver coin, delivered to Delhi by a large convoy of bullock-drawn carts, under heavy military escort. Apart from this treasure shipment however, it is possible that the Bengal authorities purchased bankers' bills (*hunḍīs*) to transfer additional or supplemental amounts to the Emperor's treasury. *See* Jadunath Sarkar, ed., *History of Bengal, Muslim Period* (Patna, 1973 reprint ed.), pp. 397–421. *See also* Mehta Balmukund, *Letters of a King-Maker of the Eighteenth Century*, edited and translated by Satish Chandra, (Aligarh, 1972), p. 39, for two letters sent by the imperial *wazīr* to Murshid Qulī Khān in 1720: the first, a reply to a report sent by Murshid Qulī Khān, commended him for personally "escorting

90 *lakhs* of treasure [nine million silver rupees] which had been loaded in carts (up to a distance of) two *kos* from the city; [and for] the appointment of Faiyyaz Ali Khan, the *bakhshi* of the *ṣūbah* [chief military officer of the province] to accompany it with your troops."

2 The usual term for a bill of exchange is *huṇḍī*, originally a Hindi word derived from the Sanskrit. *Huṅḍāwan*, the term used here, denotes the rate or price paid for a bill, that is the discount itself. Cf. Platts' *Dictionary*, p. 1237.

238b

According to the Exalted Order in the Name of the *Dīwān* of Bengal (after writing the titles)

At this time, ______ etc., bankers, in conformity with the standing order, have placed the sum of ______ *lakh* (amount, in hundreds of thousands of rupees) in the general treasury of the Stirrup of Felicity (the Emperor's camp). In compensation for this aforesaid amount of ______ rupees and the expense for discount on a bill of exchange and gratuities fixed at three months, payment has been ordered from the treasury of the Paradise of Countries, Bengal.[1] Therefore, let the most wise one (the *dīwān*) pay the aforesaid amount after deducting two *surkh*[2] in accordance with the details stipulated on the reverse.

He is to obtain a receipt bearing the seals of the bankers.

Henceforth he is to set aside as an allowance and enumerate on current account this same order (*parwāna*) and receipt (*qabẓ al-wuṣūl*). He is to know that there are strict injunctions in this matter.

Notes

1 See notes for previous order.

2 The meaning of this phrase is unclear. *Surkh* is a synonym for the *rattī*, a jeweler's and banker's weight equal to just under two English grains in the Mughal period. Steingass' Dictionary uses the same term in its other meaning, to refer simply to gold (in any amount).

238b

Order for the Cultivation of Long-untilled Land (*Banjar*) Under the Regulation for Reduced Revenues[1]

The responsible officers, present and future of ______ subdistrict, ______ district and ______ province are hereby informed that: at this time ______ has testified that the amount of waste land no longer assessable is very great in the aforesaid subdistrict, and has requested that this quantity of *bīgha* from that total may be entrusted to this slave under the regulation for reduced assessment. In return, he will sow the lands and will cause an appropriate revenue to be returned from those lands assessed at the reduced rate. He intends to promote the contentment of the populace and the settlement of that verdant country under the
239a Sublime and Resplendent Gaze (of the Emperor).

Therefore it is laid down that so many *bīgha* from the land which has fallen

out of cultivation and is outside the assessment, provided that the owner is not present, or if present is unable (to cultivate it), shall be transferred to the aforementioned person so that he shall, as far as he is able, cultivate the land and pay the following rate of tax: in the first year, one-fifth part; in the second year, one-fourth part; and in the third year, one-third part (of the total harvest). They (the officers) are not to trouble (him) in any way for other revenue, cesses or expenses.

They (the officers) must be careful not to apply the deduction for long-untilled waste lands fallen out of assessment to lands already cultivated. If future investigation reveals such a violation, they must recall and recover one half (the produce) up to the full rate of collection for sown lands. (The amount recovered must be calculated) from the date on which the delinquent taxpayer took possession of the lands to the (current) date on which the reduced rate was revealed (to be inappropriate). Let this be a warning to other persons. More than this need not be ordered.

Notes

1 The inclusion of this specimen order in this collection reflects the continuing concern of the Mughal imperial administration for keeping all the arable lands of the empire in cultivation. The administration classified as "waste" land (*banjar* or *chachar*), no longer yielding tax revenues, any villages or land left depopulated and uncultivated, whether by natural or man-made disasters, for more than a year or so. Imperial officers usually responded to this problem by reducing revenue demands and/or offering agricultural loans for entrepreneurs who would invest their energy and resources in restoring those waste areas to cultivation. Often such men attracted to the areas given them colonists of migrants from neighboring villages. The reduced assessment for the first three years of renewed cultivation is expressed in terms of the total population. That is, the rate of assessment the first year would be one-fifth of the total harvest, one-fourth the second year and one-third the third year. According to Irfan Habib, the normal practice was to raise this demand to the full one-half for grain crops in the fifth year. Cf. Habib, *The Agrarian System*, pp. 251–253. The proportions given here vary somewhat from those Habib cites for the reduced rate. Also, this document does not state whether the tax demand would be paid in kind or in cash. The mode of assessment was probably crop-sharing rather than a reduction calculated from the rate set out in the previous crop-rate schedules, outdated by the interruption of cultivation.

239a Regulation Exempting Irrigated Lands (*Bāgh*) from Taxation

They (officials) are not to disturb (the cultivators) for the purpose of revenue collection, if income (on that irrigated land) is equal to expenditure (for water), or income is less than expenditure. However, if income is greater than expenditure, they may demand one-sixth portion (of the total produce) from Muslims and one-fourth portion from Hindus. Therefore let them carry out their work in conformity with the regulation of the *ṣadr.*[1]

Notes

1 This possessive construction is not entirely clear. Possibly the regulation in question set up differential sectarian treatment in this area, which was administered by the imperial *ṣadr*, the chief religious officer for Muslim institutions and offices. Although the text is generally free from copyist's errors, this word may also have been an error for *ṣudūr* (issued, emanated).

239a Transmittal Officer (in charge of) Despatching Money and Account Papers of the Subdistrict

This order is issued to that intrepid one ______: the position of transmittal officer (*sazāwal*) officially responsible for the funds of the sublime state and for the despatch of the account papers of ______ subdistrict, ______ district and ______ province has been conferred upon
239b (him) by his solemn agreement. Therefore, he must fulfill the duties and customary obligations of this position. He must not permit the slightest matter to escape his vigilance and care. In cooperation with the *amīn* of that place, and with extreme care, he must send the accumulated revenue collections of those *maḥals*, by means of reliable merchants' bills (*hunḍūyāt*), to his Resplendent Majesty. He must also send to His Resplendent Majesty the papers for the assessment roll,[1] for receipts and arrears, etc. He must prevent any delay or procrastination in the transmittal of the papers and the money. He is to know that there are strict injunctions in this matter.

Notes

1 The *daul-jamaᶜ* listed the *jāgīrdārs'* holdings within a subdistrict or larger unit, along with the valuation assessed for each assignment.

239b Order for Monthly Salary Payment Allocated from the General Treasury

This order is issued to Sanbhunath, treasurer of the general treasury of the Stirrup of Felicity (the camp of the Emperor): in accordance with the exalted command, the sum of five hundred rupees per month is to be paid from the (funds in his) charge to the most worthy ______. (This payment) to assist with living expenses is to be made from the beginning of ______. He may pay the monthly allowance of that aforesaid *khān* in each month from the beginning of (the month) mentioned above. After taking a receipt as established by practice, he will pay the monthly salary to other stipendiaries of that place. Henceforth, in conformity with (the conditions) of this order and receipt, he will set aside and compute (that allowance) for his (the recipient's) account.

239b **Order for Payment to the Animal Stables (*Kārkhāna-i Dawābb*)**

This order is issued to ______, treasurer: he is to pay ten thousand rupees from the funds in his charge from the beginning of ______ as allowance for the feed, etc., of the horse stables, the elephant stables, or other stables for beasts in the charge of ______, the cashkeeper. Having removed the aforesaid sum from his own control and placed it in the control of the cashkeeper, ______, he must obtain a receipt bearing the seals of the officers of that aforementioned establishment. Hereafter he will make allowances for and calculate (that amount) from his accounts in
240a accordance with this present order and receipt.

240a **Order for Payment of Monthly Salary to a *Manṣabdār* from the *Maḥals* of *Sā'ir***

This order is issued to the officers of the cloth market or the Royal Market, or other *maḥals* of *sā'ir*: the sum of ______ (amount) rupees per month is to be paid from the revenues of that place to ______, *manṣabdār*, of ______ *firqat* (company) attached to the *makān* (establishment) of ______. It is decreed that they may pay the allowance of the aforementioned person commencing from ______ (date), as previously established by regulation and custom for the regular stipendiaries of that place. And they must ensure that a receipt is given to the treasurer of that place. Henceforth, in accordance with this order and receipt, (this sum) will be set aside and calculated for their account.

ساهوان

پرداخته دقیقه از دقایق حزم و هوشیاری غیر مرعی نگذارد و زر یکه از تحصیل آن محال فراهم آید
با مین آنجا تاکید نماید که بر سبیل هندویات معتبر بحضور انور ارسال دارد و کاغذ دوجمع
جمع و اصل باقی و غیره بحضور لامع النور مُعَبَر فرستاده باشد نگذارد که در ارسال کاغذ و ترسیل زر توقف
و تعلل بمیان آید در غیاب تاکید داند ه دستک تنخواه در باب دخرج مقرری از خزانه عامره

دستک باسم سبنهو باتهه خزانچی خزانه عامره رکاب سعادت انکه حسب الحکم اعلی
مبلغ پانصد روپیه در باب رفعت پناه فلان بصیغه دخرج از ابتدای فلان از تحویل او
تنخواه شده باید که او وجه در باب خانمشار الیه را از ابتدای صدر بعد گرفتن قبض الوصول
بدستور دیگر تنخواهداران مقرری آنجا موافق ضابطه ماه بماه تنخواه میداده باشد که
تا فی الحال مطابق این دستک و قبض الوصول بحساب او مجرا و محسوب خواهد شد شرح دستک
تنخواه کارخانه دواب دستک باسم فلان خزانچی انکه مبلغ ده هزار روپیه در وجه
خوراک و غیره اسپان اصطبل یا فیلان فیلخانه یا دیگر کارخانه دواب تحویل فلان تحویلدار
من ابتدای فلان از تحویل او تنخواه شده باید که مبلغ مذبور از تحویل خود بتحویل تحویلدار فلان
نموده قبض الوصول بمهر متصدیان کارخانه سطور ستاند که تا فی مطابق این دستک و قبض الوصول

درحساب

در حساب او مجرا و محسوب خواهد شد دستک تنخواه در باب منصبدار از محال دستک
باسم متصدیان کوتهه پارچه پاشاهگنج یا دیگر محال سایر آنکه مبلغ اینقدر روپیه در وجه
فلان منصبدار رفیقه فلان متعینه مکان فلان از ابتدای فلان از محصول آنجا تنخواه شده
باید که آنها وجه مشار الیه را از ابتدای صدر بدستور دیگر تنخواهداران مقرری آنجا
موافق ضابطه تنخواه میداده باشند و قبض الوصول تحویلدار آنجا بدهند که تا فی الحال
مطابق این دستک و قبض الوصول در حساب آنها مجرا و محسوب خواهد شد ۵

تنخواه حکم شده لهذا حسب الحکم اقدس اعلی قلمی میگردد که آن امارت و ایالت مرتبت
مبلغ مذکور را بموجب پروانه حضور پرنور که بنام دیوان صوبه شرف صدور یافته زود
تنخواه دهانند درینباب از جناب عالیان مآب تاکید اکید دانند حسب الحکم بنام دیوان صوبه
بنگاله بعد تحریر القاب در نیولا فلانی وغیره ساهوان مبلغ اینقدر لک روپیه بطریق دستگردان
داخل خزانه عامره رکاب سعادت نموده اند عوض آن مبلغ مذکور مبلغ اینقدر هزار روپیه وجه هندوان
و انعام شاهانه بالمقطع از خزانه صوبه جنت البلاد بنگاله تنخواه حکم شده لهذا قلمی میگردد
که آن شهامت مرتبت مبلغ مذکور را حسب الضمن بعد وضع دو سرخه بلا توقف تنخواه داده
و قبض بمهر ساهوان ستانند تا فی الحال بموجب همین پروانه قبض الوصول مجرا و محسوب
خواهد گردید درینباب تاکید دانند پروانه کاشت زمین بنجر بضابطه … متصدیان مهمات
حال و استقبال پرگنه فلان سرکار و صوبه فلان بدانند در نیولا فلانی التماس نمود که در پرگنه
مذکور زمین افتاده خارج جمع بسیار است اگر از جمله آن اینقدر بیگهه بضابطه کم دستور بطریق
استمرار حواله بنده شود آنرا مزروع ساخته محصول واجب را بسرکار مقرر گرده
میرسانیده باشد از آنجا که رفاه خلق الله و آبادی ملک منظور نظر اشرف اقدس اعلی …

لهذا قلمی میگردد که از جمله زمین بنجر افتاده خارج جمع موازی اینقدر بیگهه در صورتیکه کاشتکار
حاضر نباشد یا باوجود حضور از عهده سرانجام آن نمیتواند برآمد مشار الیه حواله نمایند که بقدر
استطاعت خود کشتکار نماید و محصول آنرا در سال اول نیم حصه و در سال دوم … چهارم حصه
و از سال سیوم حصه بطریق استمرار ازو میگرفته باشند و بعلت اخراجات دیگر مزروعه
بوجهی من الوجوه مزاحمت نرسانند و احتیاط نمایند که عوض زمین بنجر افتاده خارج جمع زمین
تواند گرفت و اگر فی الحال خلاف آن ظاهر شود از ابتدای تصرف لغایه تاریخی که خلاف
بظهور رسد کم دستور را موافق دستور محصول زمین زرعی نصف بازیافت نمایند
تا باعث عبرت دیگران گردد زیاده تاکید اکید دانند ضابطه معافی محصول اگر دخل و
خرج مساوی یا دخل از خرج کم باشد بعلت محصول مزاحمت نرسانند و اگر دخل از خرج زیاده
باشد ششم حصه از مسلمین و چهارم حصه از هنود بستانند لهذا قلمی میگردد که درینباب
موافق ضابطه صدر بعمل آرند خدمت نزاولی از سال … دستک باسم
نجابت و شجاعت … آنکه چون خدمت نزاولی تاکیدات زر سرکار معلی و ارسال کاغذ
پرگنه فلان و صوبه فلان بعهده او مقرر شده باید که بلوازم و مراسم آن خدمت قرار واقع

تقسیمی که فوت و فروگذاشت بعمل نیاید درست نموده بحضور پرنور ارسال داشته
باشد در ینباب تاکید داند خدمت داروغگی خزانه و سزاولی کاغذ صوبه دستک
باسم متصدیان مهمات صوبه فلان آنکه در ینولا حسب الحکم اعلی خدمت داروغگی
خزانه و سزاولی ارسال کاغذ صوبه مذبور از تغیر فلان بفلان مقرر شده که بلوازم مراسم آن
براستی و درستی پرداخته دقیقه از دقایق حزم و احتیاط و هوشیاری نامرعی نگذارد
و زر یکه از تحصیل برکنات و مطالبات و دیگر وجوهات فراهم آید بضابطه معهود باتفاق
دیوان صوبه و امین در خزانه نگاهدارد و در آنرا بمهر خود مقفل داشته بحضور خود و [illegible]
و بند و تقیید بکار برد که احدی دست تصرف در آن نتواند کرد و چیزی بی سند
معتبر دیوان پسند صرف نشود و سررشته کاغذ موجودات خزانه مطابق قاعده
هر پانزده روزه بحضور پرنور میفرستاده باشد و قدغن نماید که عمال محال خالصه شریفه صوبه
دو لجمع و اصل باقی و دیگر سررشته کاغذ بضابطه معین و قاعده مقرر درست نموده
بلا توقف و تاخیر بمعرفت دیوان صوبه بفرمعلی ارسال دارند و باید که [illegible]
داروغه خزانه و سزاول کاغذ آنجا دانسته مطابق برلیغ معلی بعمل آرند

237b

دستک باسم متصدیان مهمات و عمله و فعله چبوتره کوتوالی رکاب سعادت
و بلده دار الخلافه شاهجهان آباد آنکه در ینولا خدمت مشرفی بندیخانه چبوتره مذبور از تغیر
فلان بفلان مقرر شده که بلوازم و مراسم آنخدمت قرار واقعی پرداخته دقیقه از دقایق
احتیاط و هوشیاری نامرعی نگذارد و سررشته کاغذ محبوسان بشرح علت قید و سبب
خلاصی آنها موافق ضابطه نگاهدارد باید که داروغه بندیخانه دانسته لوازم و لواحق
آنرا و متعلق شناسند خدمت مردهاهی و دهیکری با نظارت دستک باسم متصدیان
مهمات و عمله و فعله فلانجا آنکه در ینولا خدمت مردهائی و دهیکری نظارت آنجا از تغیر
فلان بفلان مقرر شده که بلوازم و مراسم آن براستی و درستی پرداخته دقیقه حزم و احتیاط
نامرعی نگذارد و پیادهای متعینه آنجا را بتعهد تمام در کار پادشاهی حاضر و سرگرم نگهدارد باید
که مشار الیه را مردهها و دهیه با ناظر آنجا دانسته لوازم و لواحق آنرا متعلق شناسند
حسب الحکم بنام ناظم صوبه بنگاله بعد تحریر القاب در ینولا فلانی وغیره ساهوان مبلغ [illegible]
لک [illegible] مطابق دستگردان از خزانه عامره رکاب سعادت نموده اند و عوض آن
مبلغ مذبور [illegible] از روپیه وجه هنداوی انعام سه ماهه المقطع از خراجیت البلاد ممالک

238a

براستی و درستی پرداخته دقیقه از دقایق حزم و هوشیاری نامرعی نگذارد و
چهره خوش تحریر دیل سیاهه متصدیان آنجا میرسانیده باشد و عمله و فعله آنجا را
بحسن سلوک خود راضی داشته زیاده از رسوم مقرری چیزی از صرافان طلب ننماید
و بدعتی نو احداث نکند باید که مشار الیه را چودهری صرافه بلده مذبور دانسته
لوازم و لواحق آن را متعلق شناسند و از سخن و صلاح و صوابدید او که هر آینه
متضمن کفایت سرکار والا و رفاهیت رعایا باشد بیرون نروند خدمت مشرفی پرگنه
دستک باسم متصدیان مهمات پرگنه فلان سرکار و صوبه فلان آنکه در ینولا خدمت
مشرفی پرگنه مذبور از تغیر فلان بفلان مقرر شده که بلوازم و مراسم این خدمت
براستی و درستی پرداخته دقیقه از دقایق حزم و هوشیاری مهمل و نامرعی نگذارد
و سررشته کاغذ آنجا موافق ضابطه مقرر و قاعده معین بنحوی که هنگام تحقیق تفاوت
و تجاوز ظاهر نشود درست نموده بدفترخانه معلی میرسانیده باشد و دامی [illegible] معتبر
حضور از تحویل تحویلدار آنجا بکسی نخواهد داد و در صورت نخواهد [illegible] شناسد و
عمله و فعله را بحسن سلوک خود راضی داشته در تقدیم ضوابط این خدمت مساعی جمیله

بظهور رساند باید که آنها مشار الیه را مشرف آنجا دانسته لوازم و لواحق
این خدمت را متعلق او شناسند خدمت کروراکی خزانه و نزاولی زر اقساط پرگنه دستک
باسم متصدیان مهمات و عمله و فعله پرگنه فلان سرکار و صوبه فلان آنکه در ینولا خدمت
کروراکی خزانه و نزاولی زر اقساط پرگنه مذبور از تغیر فلان بفلان مقرر شده که بلوازم
و مراسم این خدمت براستی و درستی پرداخته دقیقه از دقایق حزم و هوشیاری
نامرعی نگذارد و محافظت خزانه بنفسه نماید که در دخل و خرج آن تفاوتی بمیان نیاید
و دامی و درمی بی سند معتبر دیوان بسیند بخرج نرود و نزاولی زر اقساط پرگنه را
بلا توقف بحضور پر نور میفرستاده باشد باید که مشار الیه را کروره خزانه و نزاول
زر اقساط پرگنه مذکور دانسته لوازم و لواحق این خدمت را متعلق او شناسند خدمت
اخبارنویسی پرگنه دستک باسم فلان آنکه در ینولا خدمت اخبارنویسی پرگنه فلان از
تغیر فلان بفلان مقرر شده که بلوازم و مراسم آن از قرار واقع پرداخته دقیقه از
دقایق حزم و هوشیاری نامرعی نگذارد و بر کیفیت معاملات و مقدمات پرگنه مذبور
بغور و جستجو تمام مطلع شده سیاهه اخبارات را بلا تفاوت و بی کم و کاست

فوت و فروگذاشتی بوقوع نیاید باید که مشارالیه را امین آنجا دانسته لوازم و لواحق
آن با متعلق شناسند خدمت پیشکاری دیوانی صوبهٔ دستک باسم متصدیان
مهمات و عمله و فعلهٔ دیوانی صوبهٔ فلان آنکه حسب الحکم اعلی خدمت پیشکاری دیوانی صوبهٔ مذکور
از تغیر فلان بفلان مقرر شده که بلوازم و مراسم آنخدمت بدیانت و راستی پرداخته
دقیقه از دقایق حزم و هوشیاری غیر مرعی نگذارد و سررشتهٔ دفتر دیوانی صوبهٔ مذکور بواقع ضبط
در دست داشته نسخهٔ دیوانی وغیره کاغذ مطلوبه را سال بسال مطابق قاعدهٔ معین بدفترخانهٔ
معلی رسانیده باشد و نوعی احتیاط و جزرسی بکار برد که در هیچ معامله از معاملات اکا
فوت و فروگذاشتی بوقوع نیاید باید که مشارالیه را پیشکار دیوانی صوبهٔ مذبور دانسته
لوازم و لواحق آن با متعلق شناسند خدمت داروغگی ناخدائی جهازات دستک باسم
متصدیان مهمات و متکفلان معاملات و عمله و فعلهٔ بندر سورت مبارک صوبهٔ زین البلاد
احمدآباد آنکه درینولا حسب الحکم اعلی خدمت داروغگی ناخدائی جهازات بندر معلی
واقعه بندر مذبور مطابق ضمن از تغیر فلان بفلان مقرر شده که بلوازم و مراسم آنخدمت باید
از راستی و درستی و امانت و دیانت قیام نموده دقیقه از دقایق حزم و هوشیاری

235b

نامرعی نگذارد و با عمله و فعلهٔ آنجا طریقهٔ حسن سلوک مسلوک دارد باید که خدمات
مذبوره بعهدهٔ مومی الیه مقرر دانسته لوازم و لواحق آن با متعلق شناسند
دست تصدی او را در اجرای امور مضافهٔ آن قوی دانند خدمت داروغگی خزانه دستک
باسم متصدیان مهمات و عمله و فعلهٔ خزانهٔ صوبهٔ فلان آنکه درینولا حسب الحکم اعلی
خدمت داروغگی خزانهٔ مذکور از تغیر فلان بفلان مقرر گشته که بلوازم و مراسم آن
بدیانت و راستی پرداخته دقیقه از دقایق حزم و هوشیاری و تهمل غیر مرعی نگذارد
و محافظت خزانه قرار واقع نموده باخبر باشد که در دخل و خرج تفاوت و نقصان نباید
و دامی بدون سند معتبر دیوان پسند صرف نشود و زریکه فراهم آید در حجرهٔ خزانه
نگاه داشته در آن را بمهر خود و خزانچی مقفل داشته بحضور خود بگشاید و ببندد و
نوعی تقید نماید که احدی دست تصرف در آن نتواند کرد باید که مشارالیه را داروغهٔ
خزانهٔ مذبور دانسته لوازم و لواحق آن با متعلق شناسند خدمت جمعداری صرافه
دستک باسم متصدیان مهمات و عمله و فعلهٔ صرافه بلده فلان آنکه درینولا خدمت
جمعداری صرافه بلدهٔ مذکور از تغیر فلان بفلان مقرر شده که بلوازم و مراسم آنخدمت

236a

محال سایر شاه گنج در کاب گنج وغیره واقعه دار الخلافه در کاب سعادت انتمه
درینولا خدمت امینی تنخواه دست بدستی روزینه داران و ماهیانه داران
و سالیانه داران آنجا از تغیر فلان بفلان مقرر شده که بلوازم و مراسم آن براستی
و درستی پرداخته دقیقه از دقایق حزم و هوشیاری غیر مرعی نگذارد و از متصدیان
محالات مذبور تنخواه جماعه مذبور گرفته بعد تنقیح صحت اسناد و حکم العالی استخلاص
و دستکهات تنخواه بمهر دیوان مصوبه موافق ضابطه دست بدست تنخواه نماید داده
باشند و قبض الوصول بمهر آنها بستاند و جمع و خرج آن را سال بسال بدفتر معلی بفرستند
باید که خانمشار الیه را امین تنخواه دست بدستی دانسته لوازم و لواحق آن
بمشار الیه متعلق شناسند میر بندری فرخنده دارو غلی نمکسار بندر دستک
باسم متصدیان مهمات بندر مبارک سورت مضافات صوبه احمد آباد آنکه درینولا
حسب الحکم اعلی خدمت میر بندری فرخنده دارو غلی نمکسار بندر مذکور از تغیر
فلان بفلان مقرر شده که بلوازم و مراسم آن خدمت براستی و درستی پرداخته
دقیقه از دقایق حزم و هوشیاری نامرعی نگذارد و سوداگران وغیره [illegible]

راضی داشته در گردآوری محصول سرکار والا آنچه لازمه تقید است بتقدیم رساند
و احتیاط بکار برد که در معاملات آنجا فوت و فروگذاشتی بوقوع نیاید باید
که مشار الیه را میر بندر آنجا دانسته لوازم و لواحق آن را متعلق بشناسند
خدمت میر بحری دارو غلی نواره دستک باسم متصدیان مهمات و عمله و فعله میر بحری
فلان جا آنکه درینولا حسب الحکم اعلی خدمت میر بحری آنجا از تغیر فلان بفلان مقرر شده
که بلوازم و مراسم آن خدمت از راستی و درستی پرداخته دقیقه از دقایق
حزم و هوشیاری غیر مرعی نگذارد و دستبهار از استحکام شب با احتیاط نگاه دارد
و تقید بکار برد که احدی از مفسدان و متمردان عبور نتواند کرد باید که مشار الیه را
میر بحر آنجا دانسته لوازم و لواحق آن را متعلق بشناسند خدمت امینی کوتوالی
دستک باسم متصدیان مهمات و عمله و فعله چبوتره کوتوالی بلده فلان آنکه
حسب الحکم خدمت امینی چبوتره کوتوالی مذکور از تغیر فلان بفلان مقرر شده که بلوازم
و مراسم آن براستی و درستی پرداخته دقیقه از دقایق حزم و هوشیاری غیر مرعی
نگذارد و با عمله و فعله آنجا سلوک پسندیده نماید و احتیاط بکار برد که در معاملات آنجا

بوجهی من الوجوه
و دارو غه نمکسار

مقرر از رو بازیافت نماید و احتیاط بکار برد که بیوپاریان هنود اجناس خود را
بنام مسلمین نتوانند نویسانید و محلکاران متعینه از دلالان آنجا بگیرد باید که آنها
مشارالله را داروغه با این آنجا دانسته لوازم و لواحق این خدمت با و
متعلق شناسند درسند خدمت کروری نقد زیاده باید نوشت که در گذر آوردی
رسد مکانات و باکه جات بروبجات نوعی تقید بکار برد که قطع رسد بنوعی نیابد
دستک توپخانه دستک باسم گماشتهای فوجداران و جاگیرداران
و گذربانان و مستحفظان طرق و شوارع آنکه فرد مهر متصدیان توپخانه سرکار والا
بدفتر معلی رسید که بموجب حکم اقدس جانوران تا بین اهتمام فلانی و غیره میرشکاران
برای گزیره برکه فلان میروند دستک حضور پرنور دربنباب مرحمت شود باید
شکار میروند که هر جا طرفداران مذکور جانوران شکار را فرود آرند لوازم چوکی و پاسبانی
بجا آورده و آنچه از گوشت و گنجشک و غیره برای طعمه مطلوب باشد بلا توقف سرانجام نموده
وجه قیمت آن موافق نرخ رو برو بدهانند و احتیاط نمایند که احدی از آنها تعدی و زور
در خانه کسی فرود نیاید و مرتکب مضرت و ایذا متنفسی نشود خدمت چوکسائی

233b

دستک باسم متصدیان مهمات و عمله و فعله دار الضرب فلانجا آنکه درینولا خدمت
چوکسائی و وزن کشی طلا و نقره محال مذکور از تغیر فلان بفلان مقرر شده که بلوازم
و مراسم آن دیانت و راستی پرداخته دقیقه از دقایق حزم و هوشیاری نامرعی
نگذارد و در رفاهیت بیوپاریان و لغایت محصول سرکار والا قرار واقعی ملحوظ داشته زر نقد و
روپیه بوزن مقرر و عیار کامل موافق ضابطه بسکه مبارک میرسانیده باشد و سوای
هشت آنه اجوره سی هزار روپیه رسوم وزن کشی و چوکسائی موافق معمول قدیم گرفته
زیاده طلبی نماید باید که مشارالله را چوکسی و وزن کش محال مذکور دانسته لوازم و لواحق آن
با و متعلق شناسند خدمت قبض نویسی منصبداران دستک باسم متصدیان مهمات و
عمله و فعله خزانه صوبه آنکه درینولا خدمت قبض نویسی منصبداران آنجا از تغیر فلان بفلان
مقرر شده که بلوازم و مراسم این خدمت از قرار واقع پرداخته دقیقه از دقایق حزم
و هوشیاری نامرعی نگذارد و قبوض منصبداران موافق ضابطه بدفتر معلی میرسانیده باشد
باید که آنها مشارالله را قبض نویس منصبداران مذکور دانسته لوازم و لواحق آن
با و متعلق شناسند خدمت امینی و داروغگی دست بدستی دستک باسم متصدیان

234a

غلات را بروقت موافق نرخ به کفایت تمام مبیع نموده زر قیمت آنرا تحویل تحویلدار نماید
و تقید بکار برد که او دامی از تحویل خود بدون سند معتبر دیوان بسند خرج نتواند کرد
و تمامی زر تحویل او را بخزانهٔ عامره رسانیده قبض الوصول با و بدهاند باید که مشار الیه را
داروغه و مستوفی غلات آنجا دانسته لوازم و لواحق آن را متعلق باو شناسند و درین باب تاکید داند
خدمت استیفار دستک باسم فلان آنکه درینولا خدمت استیفار فلانجا از تغیر
فلان باو مقرر شده که بلوازم و مراسم اینخدمت از قرار واقع پرداخته از روی راستی و
درستی در تنقیح محاسبات و مطالبات دقیقه از دقایق خبرویت و هوشیاری
غیر مرعی نگذارد و محاسبه را موافق ضابطهٔ مقرر بدستخط دیوان صوبه رساند تا بموجب
آن بازیافت و بازخواست بعمل آید درینباب تاکید داند شناسد خدمت پیشکاری دیوانی فوج
دستک باسم متصدیان مهمات و عمله و فعلهٔ دیوانی فوج همراهی فلان آنکه درینولا
خدمت پیشکاری دیوانی فوج مذبور بفلان مقرر شده که بلوازم و مراسم اینخدمت از
قرار واقع پرداخته دقیقه از دقایق حزم و هوشیاری نامرعی نگذارد و [illegible]
و دیگر ارباب طلب در خزانهٔ فوج فراهم آید احتیاط نماید که دامی بدون سند معتبر دیوان

به تنخواه در نیاید و در صورت تنخواه شدن بضابطه بازپرس آن ذمهٔ خود
شناسد و نسخه دیوانی و جمع و خرج و [illegible] خزانه و دیگر سر رشته کاغذ
موافق ضابطهٔ منقح و مفصل درست ساخته بدفترخانهٔ معلی میرسانیده باشد و
با عمله و فعله سلوک پسندیده و شایسته بکار برد باید که آنها خدمت مذکور بمشار الیه
مقرر دانسته لوازم و لواحق آن را متعلق باو شناسند داروغگی و [illegible] سایر
دستک باسم متصدیان مهمات و عمله و فعلهٔ محال سایر صوبه فلان آنکه درینولا
حسب الحکم اعلی خدمت داروغگی و امینی محال مذکور از تغیر فلان بفلان مقرر شده که بلوازم
و مراسم اینخدمت بدیانت و راستی پرداخته دقیقه از دقایق حزم و احتیاط نامرعی
نگذارد و محصول [illegible] بر طبق قاعدهٔ معین بقید ضبط در آورده بتحویلدار
نماید و محافظت و نگهبانی زر تحویل او بعهدهٔ خود دانسته نگذارد که دامی بدون سند
معتبر دیوان بجنسه صرف تواند نمود و تمامی زر تحویل در خزانهٔ عامره رسانیده قبض الوصول
باز یابد و نگهبانی خانهٔ سایر هنگام شب زیر مهر خود و داروغه نگاه دارد
و [illegible] محصول متاع خود در آنجا رسد وجه حاصل را موافق ضابطه

بجمعیت خاطر و طمانیت باطن آمد و شد نموده باشند و در هیچ جا اثری از دزدان
قطاع الطریق ظاهر نشود و اگر مال کسی به دزدی یا بغارت رود آن را بجنس یا از دزدان و رهزنان
پیدا ساخته مال را بمالک آن رسانند و در صورت پیدا نساختن از عهده
جواب مال مذبور برآید باید که چودهریان و قانونگویان و زمینداران و مقدمان و مزارعان و
رعایا را آنجا راهداری یا تهانه داری آنجا بعهده مشارالیه مقرر دانسته لوازم و لواحق آن باو
متعلق شناسند خدمت امانی تومان بشاور متصدیان مهمات و متکفلان معاملات
حال و استقبال و ملکان و مقدمان و مزارعان و رعایا تومان بشاور مضاف صوبه دار الملک کابل
بدانند که دریولا حسب الحکم اعلی خدمت امانی تومان بشاور از تغیر فلان بفلان حسب الضمن مقرر شده
که بلوازم و مراسم آن از راستی و درستی پرداخته دقیقه از دقایق حزم و هوشیاری
غیر مرعی نگذارد و در بند و بست تومان مذبور و استمالت رعایای آنجا ز بوم جد و جهد بلیغ
بظهور رساند و دیگری را بکار خود شریک و سهیم نسازد و چهل هزار روپیه پیشکش سرکار معلی در هشت سال
بقسط پنجهزار روپیه هر سال داخل خزانه صوبه مذبور سازد و در رسوم ملکانه و انعام امانی بدستور
خود بگیرد و زیاده طمع و توقع ننماید باید که خدمت مذبور بمشارالیه مقرر دانسته لوازم و لواحق آن

231b

باو متعلق شناسند و تفریق انعام و ملکانه و ناکاره و خرج الوشی و تشخیص وغیره
هرچ الوس و انعام ملکانه وغیره بشاور باستصواب مومی الیه نموده باشند
درین باب تاکید دانند خدمت داروغگی کچهری دستک باسم متصدیان مهمات و عمله و فعله
دیوانی کچهری صوبه فلان آنکه دریولا حسب الحکم اعلی خدمت داروغگی کچهری مذکور از تغیر فلان
بفلان مقرر شده که بلوازم و مراسم آن خدمت از راستی و درستی پرداخته دقیقه
از دقایق حزم و هوشیاری مهمل و نامرعی نگذارد و تقید نماید که در هیچ معامله از معاملات
آنجا فوت و فروگذاشت میان نیاید و سررشته کاغذی که از کلیات برسد از روی
آن نسخه دیوانی درست کرده بمعرفت دیوان صوبه سال بسال به فرخانه معلی رسانیده باشد
و هرچه بر ذمه هر کس مطالبه و محاسبه باشد و دیوان صوبه نوشته بدهد بتقید تمام وصول نموده
داخل خزانه عامره نماید باید که مشارالیه را داروغه کچهری دانسته لوازم و لواحق آن خدمت
باو متعلق شناسند درین باب تاکید دانند خدمت داروغگی مسبی غلات دستک باسم
متصدیان جهات و عمله و فعله فلان آنجا آنکه دریولا خدمت داروغگی مسبی غلات آنجا از
تغیر فلان بفلان مقرر شده که بلوازم و مراسم آن براستی و درستی پرداخته

232a

التوای معامله و ماندن باقی از و بازیافت خواهد شد و در بکه رعایا بنوطه خانه بیارد جهتی
آن مهر خود و دستخط فوطه دار با نهاده اند و هنگام محاسبی و اصلات را بموجب همان
جهتی با محسوب کرده اند و سوای واجب چیزی بصیغه ابواب ممنوعه نگیرد و از وجه تحصیل التحصیل خود
یکروپیه بر بصید عوض برآمد موقوف داشته داخل جمع نماید که تا فی الحال در برآمد به
او مجرا خواهد شد و ما بقی وجه مذبور بموجب سند جدا گانه منجمله زر تقاوی و تقاوی که بوصول
رسد بتصدیق امین میگرفته باشد و بر تقدیریکه زر مذبور به تنخواه حق التحصیل وفا نکند قدر را
از تحصیل سالحال بگیرد و در سررشته کاغذ موافق ضابطه بدفترخانه والا رسانیده باشد
باید که چودهریان و قانونگویان و مزارعان و رعایا آنجا مشار الیه را کروری محال مذبور
دانسته لوازم و لواحق این خدمت با و متعلق شناسند سند خدمت رفع ابواب ممنوعه
متصدیان مهمات صوبه زین البلاد احمدآباد بدانند در ینولا حسب الحکم اعلی خدمت
رفع ابواب ممنوعه واقعه صوبه مسطور از انتقال فلان بفلان مقرر شده که بلوازم و مراسم
آن براستی و درستی پرداخته دقیقه از دقایق حزم و هوشیاری نامرعی نگذارد و وجه
رفع ابواب ممنوعه آنچه لازمه تقیدست مطابق احکام شریعت غرا بتقدیم رساند

در مسجد بنا کرده قوم اسمعیلیه امام و موذن تعیین نماید و منهیات و مسکرات
برطرف سازد و از آن فریق مچلکا عدم اختلال دعوی مردم بگیرد باید که خدمت
مذبور را بالموی الیه مقرر دانسته لوازم و لواحق آن با و متعلق شناسند و در ینباب تاکید داند
سند پسر داغهای ملبوسخاص در ینولا حسب الحکم مبلغ ... دام پرگنه فلان سرکار
و صوبه فلان که از تغیر فلان ... باقی خالصه شریفه تعلق یافته من ابتدای فلان بر اسم فلان
ملبوسخاص بعهده آن قصاب مقرر شده باید که از دیاد آبادانی و تکثیر زراعت و افزونی
محصول سرکار والا و تسلی و استماله رعایا تقید بلیغ بکار برده وجه محصول آنرا از واقع
بضبط در آورده ملبوسخاص موجب برات دارد بیاغخانه درست ساخته ارسال حضور پرنور نموده باشد
در ینباب تاکید داند خدمت راهداری و تهانه داری در ینولا خدمت راهداری و تهانه داری
فلان جا متعلق صوبه فلان از تغیر فلان مطابق ضمن بفلان مقرر شده که بلوازم و مراسم این خدمت
براستی و درستی پرداخته در بند و بست و ضبط و ربط و تنبیه و تادیب مفسدان و رهزنان
[illegible] زبردستان و مالگذاران و منع اشکران بواقعی کوشد و احتیاط بکار برد
که احدی مرتکب منهیات و مسکرات نگردد و محافظت شاهراه بنوعی نماید که مسافرین و مترددین

توزیع محصول سالحال نگردد در افزونی زراعت و کثرت آبادانی مساعی موفوره بظهور
رساند و محافظت و نگاهبانی زر تحویل فوطه‌دار در جواب مبلغی که از عین المال بثبت بردا
نزد او باقی ماند بدستور مقرر بعهده خود دانسته نوعی خبردار باشد که یکدام بدون
سند معتبر دیوان پسند صرف نتواند نمود و تمامی زر تحویل در انجام امره رسانیده
قبض الوصول به فوطه‌دار بدهد و احتیاط بکار برد که به نسبت محصول عمل جاگیرداران
تفاوت بظهور نیاید و یکدام باقی نماند که در صورت التوای معامله و ماندن باقی بازخواست
آن از خواهد شد و زری که رعایا به فوطه‌خانه بیارند چتهی بمهر خود و دستخط فوطه‌دار بآنها بدهد
و هنگام مباقی و اصلات را بموجب همان چتهیها محسوب گرداند و سوای زر واجب
بصیغه ابواب ممنوعه نگیرد و از وجه حق التحصیل کروری که در عوض آن موقوف داشته
داخل جمع نماید که ثانی الحال در برآمد ذمه او مجرا خواهد شد و باقی وجه مذکور را بموجب سند
جداگانه منجمله زر تقاوی و تقاوی که بوصول رسد بدهد و بر تقدیر یکه زر مذکور تنخواه حق التحصیل وفا نکند
قدر زاید را از تحصیل سالحال تن نماید و سررشته کاغذ موافق ضابطه بدفترجات و الا رسانند
باید که چودهریان و قانونگویان و مقدمان و مزارعان و رعایای آنجا خدمت مسطور مشار الیه مقرر

229b

دانسته قول و قرار و تشخیص و پرداخت او را منظور و معتبر دانند و از سخن صلاح و صوابدید
او بیرون نروند و شکر و شکایت او را درباره خود مؤثر دانند خدمت کروری محال
پایباقی و بازیافت معاش در عهده خدمت کروری محال پایباقی و اراضی بازیافت ائمه و آبادی و معاش
پرگنه فلان سرکار و صوبه فلان از ابتدای فلان بفلان حسب الضمن مقرر شده که لوازم
و مراسم آن خدمت بدیانت و راستی پرداخته با کافه رعایا سلوک پسندیده نماید
و محالی که در پایباقی آید از اراضی واقع منضبط در آورده تا تنخواه شدن بجاگیرداران
مال واجب را موافق آنچه امین بعد ملاحظه جمع سنوات عمل جاگیرداران پیشین و موجودات
حال تجزی تمام باستصواب او مشخص نماید تحصیل نموده تحویل فوطه‌دار نماید و اگر
محالی از محالات لغایت حال نامشخص مانده باشد آن را نیز بصلاح امین تحصیل نماید و آنچه
از باقی و تقاوی سنوات نزد رعایا طلب باشد از مواضع باقیدار رجوع حال که به
تشخیص در آمد مبلغ یکدو بیست در هر فصل تحصیل در آرد و زری که بصیغه تقاوی در سال گذشته
برعایا تنخواه شده باشد یا باقی مانده بود در اول توزیع محصول سالحال بگیرد و احتیاط
بکار برد که به نسبت محصول عمل جاگیرداران تفاوت بظهور نیاید و یکدام باقی نماند که در صورت

230a

از محصول سال تحال تن نماید و بضبط محصول بنا در قرار واقعی پردازد و با تاجران سلوک
پسندیده نماید و هرگاه فصل بآخر رسد از روی کاغذ تحقیقات تغلب و تصرف
عمال نموده هرچه بنام آنها ظاهر شود بازخواست نماید و حراست حصار بندر مبارک سورت
بواقعی نماید باید که عمال و چودهریان و قانونگویان و مقدمان و مزارعان و رعایای آنجا
مشار الیه را متصدی بندر مسطور دانسته لوازم و لواحق این خدمت بومی الیه
متعلق شناسند و از سخن صلاح و صوابدید حسابی او که هر آئینه متضمن نفاست برکار
و رفاهیت رعایا باشد بیرون نروند و شکر و شکایت او را درباره خود ها
موثر دانند خدمت دیوانی فوج در نیولا حسب الحکم اعلی خدمت دیوانی فوج همراهی فلان
بفلان مقرر شده که بلوازم و مراسم این خدمت از دیانت و راستی پرداخته دقیقه
از دقایق حزم و هوشیاری مهمل و نامرعی نگذارد و زر یکجهه تنخواه سپاه و دیگر
ارباب طلب در خزانه فوج فراهم آید سربمهر و امانت داشته طلب طلبداران
بعد ملاحظه موجودات بموجب سند حضور پرنور تنخواه دهد و نوشته دیوانی را
بدون سند معتبر دیوان سند بخرج در آید و الا بازیافت و بازپرس آن آید

خود داند و نسخه دیوانی و جمع و خرج واقعه خزانه و دیگر سررشته کاغذ
موافق ضابطه و معمول به دفترخانه معلی میرسانیده باشد و با عمله و فعله و ارباب طلب سلوک
پسندیده نماید و مرتکب تعدی نشود باید که مشار الیه را دیوان فوج مذکور دانسته لوازم
و لواحق این خدمت با و متعلق شناسند خدمت امانت یا باقی در نیولا خدمت امانت یا باقی
و اراضی بازیافت ایمه ارباب مدد معاش سرکار فلان صوبه فلان از تغیر فلان بفلان حسب الضمن
من ابتدای فلان مقرر شده که بلوازم و مراسم این خدمت بدیانت و راستی پرداخته با
کافه رعایا سلوک پسندیده نماید و محالی که در باب باقی در آید از قرار واقع بضبط در آورده
تنخواه باشد بن بجاگیرداران جمع آن را بعد ملاحظه جمع سنوات عمل جاگیرداران پیشین و موجودات
حال بخبر رسی تمام بنحوی که نصف برعایا و نصف در سرکار والا برسد مشخص نموده بکروری
تاکید کند که تحصیل در آورده تحویل فوطه دار نماید و اگر احیاناً محالی از محالات بعنایه حال مشخص
نامده باشد از آنها تشخیص نموده بوصول سازند و آنچه از باقی و تقاوی سنوات در رعایا
طلب باشد از مواضع یا قید از برجمع حال که به تشخیص در آید مبلغ بتجرد به بر یکصد در هر فصل تحصیل در آید
در یکه بنصیبه تقاوی در سال گذشته برعایا تنخواه شده باشد تا باقی سالند بود در اول

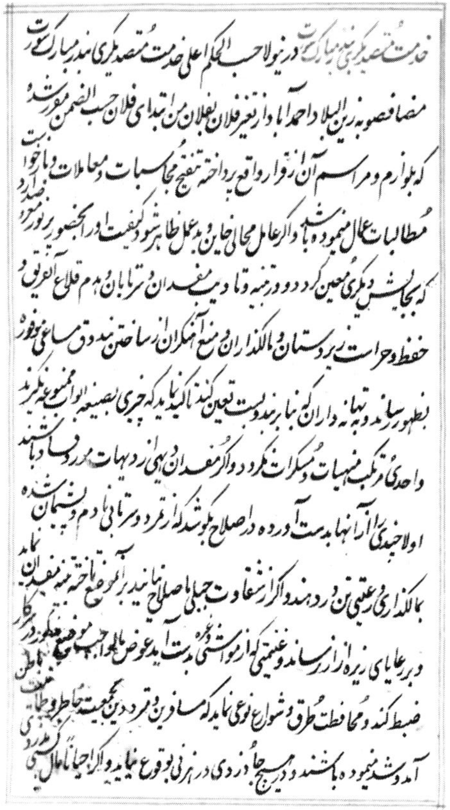

227b

228a

محلکای خدمت امانت و فوجداری مسکنه بنده درگاه خلایق پناه ام چون از پیشگاه
خلافت و جهانبانی فوجداری پرگنه فلان مضاف صوبه فلان بعهده بنده درگاه
از تغیر فلان مقرر گشته نوشته میدهم که بلوازم و مراسم آن براستی و درستی
پرداخته دقیقه از دقایق حزم و احتیاط نامرعی نگذارم و در بند و بست معاملات
و تنبیه و تادیب مفسدان و سرتابان و هدم قلاع آنفریق و حفظ و حراست زیردستان
و منع متمردان از ساختن بندوق بواقعی کوشش و جهی برائه تهانجات محال فوجداری
با ضبط و ربط تعین نمایم تاکید کنم که چیزی بصیغه ابواب ممنوعه نگیرند و احدی از آن
مرتکب منهیات و منکرات نگردد و اگر مقدمان دیهی از دیهات تمرد و فساد اختیار نماید
اولا چندی از آنجماعه بدلاسا و تسلی بدست آورده در اصلاح کوشم که از طرد
و ترتبات دم شده پاگذاری در عتبی تن در دهند و اگر از شقاوت جبلی باصلاح نیایند بر [illegible]
تاخته تنبیه مفسدان نمایم و محافظت شاهراه بنوعی نمایم که مسافرین و مترددین بجمع خاطر
و طمانیت باطن آمد و شد نموده باشند و در هیچ جا دزدی و رهزنی بوقوع نیاید و از اهل
کسی بزدی یا بغارت رود مال را بمالک و آنجماعه بدمال را بسزا رسانیم و در صورت

پیدا نساختن از عهده جواب مال بر آیم و در مال خالصه شریفه و سایر تصرف نکنم
بنابران این چند کلمه بطریق محلکا نوشته دادم که فی الحال سند باشد قبولیت
تعهد خدمت امانت و فوجداری چون خدمت امانت و فوجداری پرگنه فلان سرکار و صوبه فلان
محال خالصه شریفه من ابتدای فلان بعوض مبلغ اینقدر روپیه سکه مبارک هر سه‌ساله
هر ضربه بجهته بالعد دام ملا شرکت غیری از مالوجهات و کلجوبات لغایت فلان واجب
یکساله یا دو ساله خواه سه ساله برضا و رغبت خود قبول نمودم و اقرار مینمایم که مبلغ مذکور را بشرط
بحالی خدمت فصل بفصل بموجب اقساط ذیل در سرکار والا واصل سازم و دخل خرج زمینداری
و ناکار و غیره ابواب مخارج بدستور جاگیرداری معمول حضور اکرم و خدا نخواسته باشد اگر
آفت سماوی یا ارضی رو دهد بر وقت متصدیان سرکار اطلاع دهم و بموجب تحقیقات امین حضور
مجرا بگیرم و اگر مابین فصل یا تغیر آید بعد مجرا خرچ شبندی و غیره از روی و اصلات شان سازم
و واصلات متعهد معزول با تفاق یکدیگر از روی تحقیقات امین حضور و دستخط خود هر سال بر آن
فاضل [illegible] از تعهد خود از سرکار مجرا از قسط تمه تا دام آخر داخل نمایم بنابران این چند کلمه
بطریق [illegible] نوشته دادم که فی الحال سند باشد خریف چهار قسط و ربیع چهار قسط بود

بموجب سیاهه غله و کاغذ [illegible]

وصورت انفصال معاملات و عدم انفصال آن بقید تفصیل منعه کیفیت
و کمیت محبوسان قلعجات دکهری و سبب قید آنهارا با سوانح رو داده و
شرح آنجا از روی نفس الامر و راستی بی کم و زیاد مفصل نوشته بلا توقف
و اهمال ارسال الحضور نماید و از رعایت و عداوت محترز باشد زیاده تاکید داند
خدمت داروغگی و بهمین مضمون امینی محال زعفران دستک باسم متصدیان مهمات
و عمله و فعله محال زعفران پرگنه فلان مضافات صوبه کشمیر آنکه درینولا خدمت داروغگی
محال مذکور از تغیر فلان بفلان مقرر شده که بلوازم و مراسم آن براستی و درستی
پرداخته دقیقه از دقایق حزم و هوشیاری نامرعی نگذارد و در موسم شگفتن و چیدن
و خشک کردن و تعیین نرخ نظر بقلت و کثرت زعفران و کفایت سرکار و [illegible]
کار و بیع آن بمشتریان نهایت سعی و تقید بکار برده چنان احتیاط نماید که احدی را
مجال تغلب و تصرف نماند و وجه بهای زعفران بدستور قرارداد و صول [illegible] تقید
بکار برد که اصلا از بقیه نزد خریداران نماند باید که آنها مشار الیه را داروغه
دانسته لوازم و لواحق آن با و متعلق شناسند و [illegible] باید دانند

225b

خدمت داروغگی و بهمین مضمون امینی [illegible] دستک باسم متصدیان مهمات و
عمله و فعله منهیه نخاس بلده فلان صوبه فلان آنکه درینولا خدمت داروغگی
آنجا از تغیر فلان بفلان مقرر شده باید که بلوازم و مراسم آنخدمت بامانت و راستی
پرداخته دقیقه از دقایق حزم و هوشیاری غیر مرعی نگذارد و ضبط حاصلات
بر وفق دستور و ضابطه معین میکرده باشد و نوعی خبردار باشد که در بیع معامله
فوت و فروگذاشتی میان نیاید و احدی را مجال تصرف و تغلب نماند و [illegible]
[illegible] حبس خود را داخل امتعه مسلمین نتواند نمود و محلکاریا [illegible] از دلالان آنجا
بگیرد و محافظت و نگهبانی زر تحویل تحویلدار بعهده خود شناسد و نگذارد که تحویلدار
دامی بدون سند معتبر دیوان بسند صرف تواند نمود و تمامی زر تحویل او را بخزانه
عامره رسانیده قبض الوصول تحویلدار بدهاند باید که آنها مشار الیه را داروغه
آنجا دانسته لوازم و لواحق آنخدمت با و متعلق شناسند خدمت [illegible]
دستک باسم متصدیان مهمات محال خالصه شریفه آنکه درینولا خدمت [illegible]
[illegible] از تغیر فلان بفلان مقرر شده باید که بلوازم و مراسم آن [illegible]

226a

باید که آنها مشار الیه را کوتوال آنجا دانسته لوازم ولواحق این خدمت با متعلق
شناسند دریناب تاکید دانند خدمت مقیمی و مهتراتی در نواح حدمت
مقومی فلان محال از تغیر فلان بفلان مقرر شده که بلوازم و مراسم این خدمت از
راستی و درستی پردازد و متاعی که بیوپاریان آن محال بیارند قیمت آن را چنان
مشخص نماید که تا فی الحال در آن تفاوت ظاهر نشود و متصدیان آنجا موافق قیمت مذبور
در سرکار والا محصول آن بضبط درآرند و سوای دستور مقرری از بیوپاریان
چیزی نگیرد و بیوپاریان از حسن سلوک راضی داشته بر امور تغلب نگردد
و در خرید و فروخت چنان تقید بکار برد که نقصان بمال سرکار والا نرسد باید که
آنها او را مقوم آنجا دانسته لوازم ولواحق این خدمت با متعلق دانند در باب تاکید دانند
خدمت داروغگی جوی دستک باسم متصدیان مهمات عمله و فعله جوی آب
واقعه فلان آنجا آنکه حسب الحکم اعلی خدمت داروغگی جوی مذبور از تغیر فلان بفلان
مقرر شده که بلوازم و مراسم این خدمت بدیانت و راستی پرداخته
کشتکار جوی مذبور را بامداد رعایای دیهاتی که از جوی مذکور زراعت مینمایند

قرار واقع موافق معمول مرمت نماید که آب از جاری شود و حصه بسیه موافق زراعت
هر کدام دهات متعلقه قسمت کرده بدهد که آبادانی و افزونی محصول آن محال شود و
دولتخواهی سرکار و رفاهیت رعایا بوقوع آید باید که آنها مشار الیه را داروغه
آنجا دانسته لوازم ولواحق این خدمت با متعلق دانند خدمت داروغگی داک چوکی
دستک باسم فلان آنکه در نولا بر طبق حکم جهان مطاع آفتاب شعاع خدمت
داروغگی داک چوکی صوبه فلان از تغیر فلان با رفعت پناه مقرر و مفوض گشته باید که بلوازم
و مراسم خدمت مأموره قرار واقع پرداخته بنحوی شرایط سعی و اهتمام بجا آرد
که در رسیدن بلوه جات و غیره احکام پادشاهی توقف و تاخیر بوقوع نیاید و فرامین
سعادت آیین و احکام قدسی که متصدیان آنجا عرض صدور یابد باحتیاط رسانیده
عرایض و واقعه را مطابق دستور معمول روانه حضور پر نور نموده باشد و از
میوه را محلها بگیرد که سوای بلوه احکام نوشته غیری را همراه بلوه بحضور نیارند و از
ارتکاب اینقدر جرئت که از باب ممنوعه بارگاه والاست خدر بوده بوجهی من الوجوه
مراسم و متعرض احوال مسافرین و مترددین نشوند و سر رشته قضایای دار العدالت

نگذارد که دامی بدون سند معتبر دیوان پسند بخرج تواند رفت باید که آنها او را
را این انحال دانسته لوازم و لواحق انخدمت با و متعلق دانند یاده تاکید دانند
خدمت صاحب عیاری دار الضرب دستک باسم متصدیان مهمات و عمله و فعله دار الضرب
واقعه صوبه فلان آنکه در نیولا خدمت صاحب عیاری محال مذبور از تغیر فلان بفلان
مقرر شده باید که بلوازم و مراسم انخدمت قرار واقع از راستی و درستی پرداخته
دقیقه از دقایق حزم و هوشیاری نامرعی نگذارد و اشرفی و روپیه و غیره بعیار کامل
موافق ضابطه مقرر بسکه مبارک رساند باید که آنها مشار الیه را صاحب عیار
آنجا دانسته لوازم و لواحق انخدمت با و متعلق شناسند خدمت چودهرائی
محال سایره دستک باسم متصدیان مهمات و عمله و فعله محال سایر پرگنه فلان
صوبه فلان آنکه در نیولا خدمت چودهرائی محال مذبور بقبول پیشکش انقدر زر به
سرکار والا از تغیر فلان بفلان مقرر گشته که بلوازم و مراسم انخدمت قرار واقع
پرداخته دقیقه از دقایق حزم و احتیاط نامرعی نگذارد و بیوپاریان را از حسن سلوک
خود راضی داشته پیرامون تغلب نگردد و در دولتخواهی و کار آوری محصول

223b

سرکار والا انچه لازمه تقیدست بتقدیم رساند باید که آنها خدمت مذبور را
بمشار الیه مقرر و مفوض دانسته لوازم و لواحق انخدمت با و متعلق شناسند و
در مهمات تاکید دانند خدمت کوتوالی کاب دستک باسم متصدیان مهمات
و عمله و فعله چبوتره کوتوالی کاب سعادت یا بلده فلان صوبه فلان آنکه در نیولا
حسب الحکم اعلی خدمت کوتوالی بلده مذبور از تغیر فلان بفلان مقرر شده که لوازم
و مراسم انخدمت از راستی و درستی پرداخته دقیقه از دقایق حزم و
هوشیاری نامرعی نگذارد و از احوال سکنه آنجا بواقعی خبردار بوده در ضبط و
ربط و محافظت شهر و پاسبانی شب سعی فراوان بکار برد و نوعی بندوبست نماید
که دزدی نشود و در صورت وقوع دزدی سارقان را با مال پیدا ساخته مال را
بمالک و دزدان بسزا رساند و الا از عهده آن جواب گوید و تقید بکار برد که
احدی مرتکب جور و تعدی نشود و مسکرات و منهیات بعمل نیاید و جمعی که بخباثت
گرفتار آیند در باره حبس و خلاص آنها بنحوی که قاضی آنجا برفق حقیقت آنجا حکم
دستخط کند بعمل آرد و سکنه شهر و عمله و فعله چبوتره کوتوالی سلوک پسندیده نماید

224a

باسم متصدیان مهمات محال سایر فلان صوبه فلان آنکه در ینولا خدمت
تحویلداری محال مذبور از تغیر فلان بفلان مقرر شده که بلوازم و مراسم آنخدمت
بدیانت و راستی تمام پرداخته دقیقه از دقایق حزم و احتیاط نامرعی
نگذارد و زر یکه تحویل او شود با احتیاط تمام در کوتهه زیر مهر خود داردو
نگاهداشته دامی بدون سند معتبر دیوان بسند خرج نکند و تمامی زر تحویل خود
باستصواب امین بخزانه عامره رسانیده قبض الوصول بگیرد باید که موی الیه را
تحویلدار آنمحال دانسته لوازم و لواحق آنخدمت با و متعلق دانند و آنچه از محصول آنمحال
بوصول درآید تحویل او نموده چیزی علحده نگاهدارند خدمت مشرفی محال سایر
دستک باسم متصدیان مهمات مال سایر فلان متعلقه صوبه فلان آنکه در ینولا
خدمت مشرفی آنجا از تغیر فلان بفلان مقرر شده که بلوازم و مراسم آنخدمت
براستی و درستی پرداخته دقیقه از دقایق حزم و احتیاط غیر مرعی نگذارد و کاغذ
موافق ضابطه مقرر و قاعده معین درست ساخته بدفترخانه معلی رسانیده باشد
باید که انها او را مشرف آنجا دانسته لوازم و لواحق آنخدمت با و متعلق

خدمت پیشکاری فوجداری [illegible] دستک باسم زبده الاماثل والاقران آنکه در ینولا خدمت
پیشکاری فوجداری و امینی محال فلان از تغیر فلان بفلان مقرر شده باید که بلوازم و
مراسم آن بدیانت و راستی از قرار واقع پرداخته دقیقه از دقایق حزم
و هوشیاری غیر مرعی نگذارد و در جمیع معاملات آنجا نوعی خبردار
بکار برد که فوت و فروگذاشت دامی بوقوع نیاید و سررشته کاغذ را موافق
ضابطه بر طبق قاعده معین و مقرر مفصل و منقح درست کرده بدفترخانه معلی رسانیده
باشد در نیباب تاکید داند خدمت داروغکی و امینی دار الضرب دستک باسم
متصدیان مهمات و عمله و فعله دار الضرب واقعه صوبه فلان آنکه در ینولا حسب الحکم
خدمت داروغکی محال مذبور از تغیر فلان بفلان مقرر شده که بلوازم و مراسم آنخدمت
بدیانت و راستی پرداخته دقیقه از دقایق حزم و احتیاط نامرعی نگذارد و
در تقید بکار برد که محصول آنمحال بضابطه مقرر و قاعده معین بضبط درآید و فوت
و فروگذاشت نشود و اشرفی و روپیه وغیره خوش خط و بوزن و عیار کامل بسکه مبارک
مسکوک میشده باشد و محافظت و نگهبانی زر تحویل خزانچی بعهده خود دانسته

221b

واحتیاط غیر مرعی نگذارد و برآمد عمال معزول از روی کاغذ خام اصلی که مبرا
از شائبهٔ تلبیس باشد بدقت تمام بنحوی که حرفی پوشیده و پنهان نماند و
بر احدی از عاملان حیف و میل نرود و بمواجههٔ گماشتهٔ عمال باتفاق داروغه
تحقیق آورده طوامیر آنرا بضابطهٔ مقرر درست ساخته بتصدیق داروغه
خود و بدستخط چودهریان و قانونگویان بدفتر معلی ارسال دارد تا بموجب آن
بازخواستی و بازیافتی که از هر کدام باید نمود بعمل درآید باید که آنها مشارالیه
را برآمدنویس آنمحال دانسته لوازم و لواحق اینخدمت با و متعلق دانند
و در احضار و ارجاع چودهریان و قانونگویان و مقدمان و دیگر عمله و فعله و گماشته
کاغذی که جهة تفتیش اینمعامله درکار باشد توقف نکنند و رفاقت و همراهی مشارالله
در سرانجام اینکار بوجه احسن نمایند پروانهٔ بیاض امانت و فوجداری رعیت پناه و شجاعت و
امانت دستگاه محفوظ باشند درینولا حسب الحکم اشرف اقدس اعلی خدمت
امانت و فوجداری پرگنهٔ فلان سرکار و صوبهٔ فلان من ابتدای فلان بتغیر فلان بافلان
مقرر و مفوض شده باید که شکرانهٔ این موهبت عظمی بجا آورده دقیقه [illegible]

222a

رعایا و حفظ و حراست زیردستان و مالگذاران و گردآوری مال واجب
سرکار معلی و افزونی زراعت و کثرت معموری مساعی جمیله بکار برد و مال واجب را
بروقت و هنگام معرض تشخیص و تحصیل درآورده برسبیل هندویات صرافان
معتبر بحضور پرنور ارسال داشته باشد متعاقب وکیل از رفعت پناه سند ضمنی حاصل
کرده خواهد فرستاد خدمت داروغگی خزانه پرگنه دستگاه [illegible] متصدیان مهمات
خزانهٔ پرگنهٔ فلان سرکار و صوبهٔ فلان آنکه درینولا حسب الحکم اعلی داروغگی خزانه مذبور از
تغیر فلان بفلان مقرر شده که بلوازم و مراسم اینخدمت بدیانت و امانت پرداخته دقیقه
از دقایق حزم و هوشیاری غیر مرعی نگذارد و محافظت خزانه کما ینبغی نماید و زر که درا
آید در خزانه نگاه داشته در آنرا بمهر خود و خزانچی مقفل داشته بحضور خود بکشاید و بر بندد و
زر را بقاعدهٔ معین و مقرر باحتیاط تمام مصحوب جمعیت فوجدار بخزانهٔ عامرهٔ صوبه رسانیده
باشد و قبض بخط خزانچی باشد و تقید بکار برد که دامی بدون سند معتبر دیوانی بسند صرف نشود
و احدی دست تصرف دراز نتواند کرد باید که مشارالیه را داروغهٔ خزانهٔ مذبور
دانسته لوازم و لواحق اینخدمت با و متعلق دانند خدمت تحویلداری محال دستک

دقایق حزم و هوشیاری نامرعی نگذارد و موازنه و دستور العمل و دیگر
سررشته کاغذ حالی اصل و جمعدامی وغیره موافق ضابطه و معمول سال بسال
معرفت دیوان صوبه بدفترخانه والا میرسانیده باشد و بدعت احداث
ننماید و رعایا و برایا و دیگر سکنه آنجا را بحسن سلوک راضی داشته
برامون تغلب و تعدی نگردد و چیزی از کسی سوای رسوم مقرری که طمع و توقع
ننماید باید که چودهریان و قانونگویان و مقدمان و رعایای مشار الیه را قانونگوی
آنجا دانسته از سخن حسابی و صلاح و صوابدید او که هر آینه متضمن کفایت سرکار والا
و رفاهیت رعایا باشد بیرون نروند و درین باب تاکید دانند
متصدیان مهمات و متکفلان معاملات و چودهریان و قانونگویان و مقدمان
پرگنه فلان سرکار صوبه فلان بدانند که در ینولا حسب الحکم اعلی خدمت زمینداری
محال المسطور مطابق ضمن از تغیر فلان بتقول مبلغ اینقدر روپیه مشتمل سرکار
بفلان مقرر شده که بلوازم و مراسم آن از قرار واقع پرداخته با کافه رعایا
برایا سلوک پسندیده نماید و در اخراج و تنبیه و تادیب مفسدان ...

موفوره بظهور رساند و چنان کند که اثری از دزدان و رهزنان در آن سرزمین
باقی نماند و در تسلی و استمالت رعایا و افزونی زراعت و ازدیاد آبادی و اظهار
مراسم دولتخواهی کوشش فراوان بکار برد و نوعی بندوبست نماید که مفسدان
متمرد را اصلا مجال مداخلت در آن محال نباشد و از شاهراه نوعی خبردار باشد که
مسافرین و متردّدین بجمعیت خاطر و طمانیت باطن آمد و شد نموده باشند و در
هیچ جا دزدی و رهزنی بوقوع نیاید و اگر مال کسی بدزدی یا بغارت رود
دزدان و رهزنان را پیدا ساخته مال را بمالک و آنجاعه بدمال را بسزا رساند و در صورت
پیدا نساختن از عهده جواب مال مذبور برآید و تقید نماید که احدی در حدود متعلقه
زمینداری او مرتکب منهیات و مسکرات نگردد و باید که مشار الیه را زمیندار محال
مرقوم دانسته لوازم و لواحق این خدمت را متعلق و دانند خدمت برآمد نویسی
متصدیان مهمات سرکار صوبه فلان بدانند که در ینولا حسب الحکم اعلی خدمت
برآمد نویسی محال المعزول آنجا از تغیر فلان بفلان مطابق ضمن مقرر شده که بلوازم
و مراسم این خدمت بدیانت و راستی قیام نموده دقیقه از دقایق حزم

برآمد ابواب جمع نماید و تتمه را منجمله زر که از بقایا و تقاوی بوصول رسد بتصدیق
امین بگیرد و زر که از بقایا و تقاوی سنوات که از سنه چهل و دو عهد حضرت خلد مکان
نزد رعایا باقی باشد از مواضع باقیدار برجمع حال که امین تشخیص نماید بتجویز دیوان بتصدیع بر مال در
هر فصل باتفاق امین بوصول رساند و زر که بصیغه تقاوی در سال گذشته از سرکار والا
برعایا تنخواه شده باشد در اول توزیع محصول سال حال بگیرد و بر نقد اجمال بابت اجرا
آن بعهده خود شناسد و هر قدر زر رعایا به فوطه خانه بیارد جهتی آن مهر خود
و دستخط فوطه دار بآنها بدهد و بهنگام میباقی و اصلات را موافق
همان جهتها محسوب گرداند و سوای زر واجب چیزی بصیغه بهنت و تحصیلداری
و دیگر ابواب ملبه نگیرد و مجمل و جمع و خرج دیگر سررشته کاغذ را موافق ضابطه و
معمول بدفترخانه معلی میرسانیده باشد باید که چودهریان و قانونگویان و مقدمان و
رعایا و مزارعان آن محال مشار الیه را گروری آنجا دانسته لوازم و لواحق آن خدمت
با و متعلق دانند خدمت فوطه داری درینولا خدمت فوطه داری پرگنه فلان سرکار فلان
از تغیر فلان مطابق ضمن من ابتدای فلان بفلان مقرر شده که بلوازم و مراسم آن خدمت

219b

براستی و درستی پرداخته دقیقه از دقایق حزم و هوشیاری و احتیاط
غیر مرعی نگذارد و زر که از محصول آنجا فراهم آید باحتیاط تمام در حجره
فوطه خود نگاه داشته و در آن را بمهر خود و امین مقفل داشته باتفاق
یکدیگر بگشاید و بربندد و یکدام بی سند معتبر دیوان بی سند بخرج نیارد
و تمامی زر تحویل خود را باستصواب امین در خزانه عامره رسانیده قبض الوصول
بگیرد باید که متصدیان مهمات آنجا مومی الیه را فوطه دار آن محال دانسته
لوازم و لواحق آن خدمت با و متعلق شناسند و هر چه بتحصیل درآید رو در
تحویل او نموده چیزی علحده نگاه ندارند درینباب تاکید دانند خدمت چودهرائی
و قانونگوئی متصدیان مهمات و متکفلان معاملات حال و استقبال بدانند
که درینولا حسب الحکم اعلی خدمت چودهرائی قانونگوئی پرگنه فلان از تغیر فلان بن
بقبول [illegible] مبلغ [illegible] پیشکش سرکار معلی مطابق ضمن مقرر و مفوض شده که بلوازم
و مراسم آن [illegible] قیام نموده در دولتخواهی و کفایت سرکار والا و آبادی
و استمالت رعایا و افزونی زراعت مساعی جمیله بظهور رسانیده دقیقه از

220a

سالحال تن نماید و دو لجمع و دیگر سررشته کاغذ هر فصل را درست کرده بحضور پر نور
میفرستاده باشد باید که چودهریان و قانونگویان و مقدمان و رعایا و مزارعان آنجا
مومی الیه را فوجدار و امین آنمحال دانسته از سخن صلاح و صوابدید شان که هر آینه متضمن بهبود دولت
در انجام معاملات و کفایت سرکار والا و رفاهیت رعایا و مالگذاران و تقاوی آبادی بوده باشند
[illegible] لوازم و لواحق آن خدمت با و متعلق شناسند فوجداری جاگیر در نولا
حسب الحکم اعلی خدمت فوجداری دامهای جاگیر فلان که در پرگنه فلان سرکار و صوبه فلان
تنخواه است حسب الضمن از تغیر فلان بعهده فلان مقرر شده باید که بلوازم و مراسم آن از
قرار واقع پرداخته و در ضبط و ربط و تنبیه و تادیب مفسدان و سرتابان و هدم قلاع آنفریق
و حفظ و حراست زیردستان و مالگذاران و منع آهنگران از ساختن بندوق کوشد و اقعی
کوشد و جمعی که به تهانجات محال فوجداری بواسطه بند و بست و ضبط و ربط تعین کند
تاکید نماید که چیزی بصیغه ابواب ممنوعه نگیرند و احدی مرتکب منهیات و مسکرات نگردد
و اگر مفسدان دیهی از دیهات آنمحال مصدر فساد باشند اولا چندی برا از آنجا عه بدست
آورده در اصلاح بکوشد که از تمرد و سرتابی نادم شده بمالگذاری و رعیتی تن در دهند

218b

و اگر از شقاوت جبلی باصلاح نیاید بر او ضع تاخته تنبیه مفسدان نماید و در زره عایا را
آزار نرساند و بندی نکند مگر در دار الحرب و محافظت شاهراه نوعی نماید که مسافرین
و متردّدین بجمعیت خاطر و طمانیت باطن آمد و شد مینموده باشند و در هیچ جا دزدی
و رهزنی بوقوع نیاید و اگر احیانا مال کسی دزدی یا بغارت رود دزدان و رهزنان را
پیدا ساخته مال را بمالک و آنجا عه بد مال را ابزار سانده و در صورت پیدا ساختن از
عهده جواب مال مزبور برآید باید که چودهریان و قانونگویان و رعایا و مقدمان و مزارعان
آنجا مومی الیه را فوجدار محال جاگیر مسطور دانسته لوازم و لواحق آن خدمت با و متعلق دانند
و در هیچ باب تاکید شناسند خدمت کروڑگیری در نولا حسب الحکم اعلی خدمت کروڑگیری
پرگنه فلان سرکار و صوبه فلان از تغیر فلان مطابق ضمن از ابتدای فلان بفلان مقرر شده
باید که بلوازم و مراسم آن براستی و درستی پرداخته در ازدیاد آبادانی و افزونی و معموری
و کثرت زراعت و فراهم آوردن رعایا بواقعی کوشد و محصول و حقوق دیوانی آنمحال را مطابق
تشخیص امین ماه بماه و آخر بوصول آورده بخزانه تحویل فوطه دار نماید و یکدام علیحده نگاه دارد
و از اخذ ابواب طلبه و وجوه ممنوعه محترز و مجتنب باشد و منجمله حق التحصیل خود دیگر عوض

219a

217b

فساد باشند و عامل درباره تنبیه آنها نوشته بدهد اولاً چندی را از آنها
بدست آورده در اصلاح بکوشد که از تمرّد و سرتابی نادم شده بمالگذاری و زراعت تن
در دهند و بر تقدیر اصلاح رضانامه از عامل بگیرد و اگر از شقاوت جبلی باصلاح نیایند
بر موضع کوه تاخته تنبیه مفسدان نماید و رعایای ریزه را ایذا نرساند و غنیمتی که از مواشی
وغیره بدست آید از ابعامل تسلیم نموده قبض بگیرد یا از عوض مال واجب موضع بور در
سرکار ضبط نماید و بندی نکند مگر در دار الحرب و محافظت طرق و شوارع بنوعی نماید
که مسافرین و متردّدین بجمعیت خاطر و طمانیت باطن آمد و شد مینموده باشند و در
هیچ جا دزدی و رهزنی بوقوع نیاید و اگر احیاناً مال کسی بدزدی و یا بغارت رود
آنرا با دزدان و رهزنان پیدا ساخته مال را بمالک و اگر جماعه بدمال را بسزا رساند و در
صورت پیدا نساختن از عهده جواب مال مذبور برآید و احتیاط نماید که منهیات و مسکرات
در آن محال بعمل در نیاید و در تسلی و استمالت رعایا و افزونی زراعت هر موضع سعی نماید
و بر ربیع هر جنس مطلع شده جمع را هر سال از روی جزرسی بعد ملاحظه مزروعات
بدهی و دریافت احوال رعایا بنوعی که بر ریزه رعایا سختی نرود و گنجایش در تحصیل

218a

نماند و نصف سالم برعایا و نصف بی نقصان بسرکار والا رسد تشخیص نموده بکروری
تاکید کند که تحصیل درآورده تحویل فوطه دار نماید و زریکه از سنه چهل و دو جلوس حضرت خلد مکان
نزد رعایا باقی باشد بکروری قدغن نماید که بتصدیق بخرج و به برجع حال که بتشخیص در آید در هر فصل
تا وصول آن تحصیل درآورد و آنچه بصیغه تقاوی در سال گذشته برعایا تنخواه شده باشد
آنرا با باقی سالها بور در اول توزیع سال الحال بگیرد که در صورت اهمال بازخواست از او
خواهد شد و احتیاط بکار برد که کروری جرات باخذ طلبه و وجوه ممنوعه بارگاه والا نکند
و محافظت زر تحویل فوطه دار و بازخواست مبلغی که از عین المال یا برداشت که زرد
او باقی باشد مطابق دستور مقرر بعهده خود شناسد و باخبر باشد که فوطه دار یکدام
بی سند معتبر دیوان بسند خرج نکند و زر مسطور را بخزانه عامره رسانیده قبض الوصول
آن به فوطه دار بدهد و بر طبق قاعده معین از وجه حق التحصیل کروری بگیرد و بعوض برآمد
موقوف داشته داخل درجمع نماید که تا فی الحال در برآمد کروری مجرا شده و باقی را
بموجب ضبط خود مضبوط منجمله بقایا و تقاوی که بوصول رسد بتصدیق خود کروری تنخواه
میداده باشد و بر تقدیریکه زر مسطور بتنخواه حق التحصیل وفا نکند قدر زاید را از تحصیل

که مطابق آن بعرض اشرف اقدس رسید و بجای او دیگری از حضور معین گردد و اصلا
بی حکم والا اجرات تغیر و تبدیل نکند و هر عاملی که معزول شود باز یافت و باز خواستی که از و
باید کرد روبرو کرده بحضور بفرستد که آمده محاسبه بگذراند و از راه احتیاط در
هر فصل از هر پرگنه کاغذ چند دیه گرفته برجان(?) جاری کند اگر از روی آن ظاهر شود که عامل
زری از ابواب ممنوعه و وجوه طلبه متصرف شده اند رو برو از آنها باز خواست کند و
ترجمان الحضور ارسال دارد که در خور کردار بسزا رسیده در حبس مقید باشد تا متعلمان(?)
دیگر عبرت گیرند و در صورت عدم ظهور تصرف عامل را اگر خدمت دارد و نسخه دیوانی
طومار و دیگر کاغذ از فصل بفصل سال بسال بقاعده معینه بدفترخانه معلی رسانیده باشد
و از چودهریان و قانونگویان مچلکا بگیرد که بر تقدیر تصرف عاملان در ابواب ممنوعه حقیقت
حال ظاهر نمایند و اگر در اظهار آن مداهنه و مساهله ورزند عرضداشت نماید که آنها از خدمات
معزول گردیده از موطن و مسکن اخراج یابند و معتبر سازد که منجمله بقایا و تقاوی که از
سنه چهل و دو عهد حضرت خلد مکان نزد رعایا طلب باشد از مواضع با قید ابراز جمع حال
که امنا تشخیص آن نموده باشند مبلغ پنج روپیه بری یکصد روپیه در هر فصل عاملان محال

بوصول رسانند و زریکه بصیغه تقاوی در سال گذشته از سرکار والا تنخواه شده باشد آنرا
با باقی رسالند(?) بور در اول توزیع محصول سالحال بگیرد و از وجه حق التحصیل کرویان مگیرد
برسید با عوض برآمد موقوف داشته تمه را منجمله بقایا بموجب اسناد علحده مسدود
باشد و اگر احیانا وجه مذکوره به تنخواه حق التحصیل وفا نکند قدر زاید را از محصول سالحال
تنخواه نماید باید که متصدیان مهمات انجا مومی الیه را دیوان مستقل دانسته لوازم و
لواحق آن بمشارالیه متعلق شناسند و دست احدی و را در اجرای امور مصالحه
و متعلقه آن قوی دانند و درین باب تاکید دانند خدمت فوجداری و امانت در سوانح حسب الحکم اعلی
خدمت فوجداری و امانت سرکار فلان صوبه فلان از تغیر فلان بفلان من ابتدا
فصل فلان حسب الضمن مقرر و مفوض گشته که بلوازم و مراسم آن خدمت از قرار واقع
دقیقه از دقایق حزم و احتیاط غیر مرعی نگذارد و در ضبط و ربط و تنبیه و تادیب متمردان
و حرامیان و هدم قلاع آنها و حفظ و حراست بر دستان و پالگذاران و منع امتلا زن
از ساختن بندوق مساعی جمیله بکار برد و بهانه داران که بواسطه ضبط و ربط تعین کنند
قدغن نماید که چیزی بصیغه ابواب ممنوعه نگیرند و از مفسدان دیهی از دیهات آنمحال مورد

شرح اسناد خدمات موافق دفتر والا

شرح صوبه داری

خدمت صوبه داری بموجب فرمان والاشان مقرر میشود و سند نیابت آن
از دفتر والا در خالصه شریفه قلمی می آید حسب الحکم اعلی خدمت نیابت صوبه داری صوبه فلان
که اصالتاً به امارت مرتبت فلان مقرر شده بشهامت و عوالی منزلت فلان تفویض یافته
باید که در نظم و نسق و تمشیت مهمات آن صوبه و محافظت و محارست بلاد و امصار و تنبیه و
تادیب مفسدان و سرکشان و قلع و قمع بنیه فتنه انگیزان و امنیت طرق و شوارع و امداد
و اعانت فوجداران و امنای محال خالصه شریفه و بازیافت باقی و کمک شتهای جاگیرداران
و عدم اخذ ابواب ممنوعه بارگاه معلی و رفع و دفع منهیات و مسکرات سعی و اهتمام
بلیغ بجا آورد و تقید تمام بکار برد که احدی از اقویا دست تعدی بحال ضعفا دراز
نتواند کرد باید که منصبداران مهمات و عمال و فوجداران خان مشارالیه را نایب ناظم
آن صوبه دانسته دست تصرف او را در اجرای امور مضافه آن قوی شناسند
و از سخن و صلاح و صوابدید حسابی خان موما الیه بیرون نروند و خدمت دیوانی صوبه
حسب الحکم اعلی خدمت دیوانی صوبه فلان از تغیر فلان بفلان از ابتدای فصل فلان

215b

حسب الضمن مقرر و مفوض گشته که بلوازم و مراسم خدمت مذکور بدیانت
و راستی به پردازد و در پرداخت محال خالصه شریفه آن صوبه و تسلی و استماله
رعایا و ازدیاد آبادانی و افزونی معموری و تکثیر زراعت دقیقه از دقایق
نامرعی نگذارد و آنچنان نماید که تعدی از عمال در اخذ خراج زیاده از نصف
باندازه و طریقه که در شرع انور و ملت حنیفه اطهر مقرر گشته از رعایا طلب نکنند
تا نقصانی و ضرری برعایا نرسد و گنجایش در تعلقات زمینداران متغلب
نگذارد و از عمال و کروریان و فوطه داران خبردار بوده دست تغلب و تصرف
آنها کوتاه دارد و قدغن نماید که هیچیک از عمال الصیغه نهیب و بالادستی و تحصیلداری
و تنبه داری و خرج صادر و وارد و دیگر ابواب که بمقتضای رعیت پروری از
پیشگاه مرحمت گستری معاف شده از رعایا طلب ننماید و اگر شخصی از عمال دست
تصرف به ابواب مذکوره و وجوه معفوه دراز کند یا سستی در تحصیل نماید حقیقت او را
از روی نفس الامر حق بنوعی که اگر ثانی الحال تفتیش آن بمیان آید خلاف
ظاهر نشود و مجمول بر اغراض نفسانی که در کار باندموم است نگردد و بموجب

216a

فهرست شرح اسناد خدمات اهلکارات و ارباب طلب جمله شصت و پنج سند

صوبه داری بموجب فرمان والاشان	نیابت صوبه داری	دیوانی صوبه	فوجداری و امانت محالات
فوجداری جاگیر	کروری محالات	قوطه داری پرگنه	چودهرائی و قانونگوئی
زمینداری	برآمدنویسی پرگنه	پروانه بیاض امانت و فوجداری	داروغگی خزانه پرگنه
تحویلداری محال سایر	مشرفی محال سایر	پیشکاری امانت و فوجداری پرگنه	داروغگی و امینی دارالضرب
صاحب عیاری دارالضرب	چودهرائی محال سایر	کوتوالی بلده	معینی و مهرائی
داروغگی جوی آب	داروغگی دکچوکی	داروغگی و امینی محال زعفران	داروغگی و امینی پنبه نخاس
پیمانه کشی	محلکا خدمت امانت و فوجداری	قبولیت تعهد خدمت امانت و فوجداری	متصدی گری سورت بندر مبارک
دیوانی فوج	امانت پایباقی	کروری محال پایباقی و بازیافت اراضی [illegible]	خدمت رفع ابواب ممنوعه
سیر دواهای ملبوس خاص	راهداری و نهانه داری	خدمت [illegible] تومان پشاور	داروغگی کچهری

داروغگی مستغلات	خدمت استیفا	پیشکاری توپخانه فوج	داروغگی و امینی سایر
دستک و سخانه برای [illegible]	جوکسائی [illegible] دارالضرب	قبض نویسی منصبداران	امینی تنخواه دستک روزینه داران [illegible]
میربندری فرضه و داروغگی [illegible] بندر	میربحری و داروغگی نواره	امینی کوتوالی	پیشکاری دیوان صوبه
داروغگی و ناخدائی جهازات	داروغگی خزانه صوبه یا پرگنه	چودهرائی صرافه	مشرفی پرگنه
کروری خزانه و نزاولی [illegible] پرگنه	اخبارنویسی پرگنه	داروغگی خزانه و نزاولی کاغذ صوبه	مشرفی بندخانه
مردمانی [illegible] با نظارت [illegible]	حسب الحکم نام ناظم صوبه درتنخواه دستکروان ساهوان	پروانه بنام فوجدار صوبه بنگاله درتنخواه [illegible]	پروانه کاشت زمین [illegible] دستور
پروانه ضابطه معافی محصول تنباکو	نزاولی ارسال کاغذ پرگنه	دستک تنخواه ساهوان مدد خرج [illegible]	دستک تنخواه کارخانجات دواب خزانه
دستک تنخواه [illegible] منصبداران از محال سایر			